61

D0853270

Merger and Competition Policy
in the
European Community

De Vries Lectures in Economics

Professor F. de Vries (1884–1958) became the first professor of economics at the Netherlands School of Economics (Rotterdam), which was founded in 1913. In 1945 he accepted an offer from the University of Amsterdam to teach economics in its Faculty of Law. On May 2, 1954, the occasion of his seventieth birthday, his pupils created the Professor F. de Vries Foundation to honor a most influential teacher, and a scholar of outstanding theoretical and practical wisdom.

The aim of the foundation is to regularly invite prominent economists from abroad for a series of lectures on theoretical subjects, as a stimulus to theoretical work in economics in the Netherlands.

F. de Vries Foundation

Merger and Competition Policy
in the
European Community

ALEXIS JACQUEMIN ET AL.

Edited by
P. H. ADMIRAAL

Basil Blackwell

First published 1990
First published in USA 1991

Basil Blackwell Ltd
108 Cowley Road, Oxford, OX4 1JF, UK

Basil Blackwell, Inc.
3 Cambridge Center
Cambridge, Massachusetts 02142, USA

British Library Cataloguing in Publication Data
A CIP catalogue record for this book is available from the British Library.

Library of Congress Cataloging in Publication Data
Merger and competition policy in the European Community/edited by P. H. Admiraal.
p. cm.
Papers from the seminar "Merger control in the EC" held in Rotterdam, autumn, 1989, sponsored by the Professor F. de Vries Foundation.
Includes bibliographical references and index.
ISBN 0–631–17832–5 (hardback)
1. Consolidation and merger of corporations—Government policy—
European Economic Community countries—Congresses.
2. Competition—Government policy—European Economic Community countries—Congresses.   I. Admiraal, P. H.
II. Professor F. de Vries Foundation.
HD2844.5.M47   1990
338.8′3′094—dc20   90–904
                                              CIP

Typeset in 12 on 14 pt Garamond
by Graphicraft Typesetters Ltd, Hong Kong
Printed in Great Britain by
Billing & Sons Ltd, Worcester

3

Contents

Notes on Contributors

A. P. Jacquemin is professor of economics at the Catholic University of Louvain-la-Neuve, Belgium and director of the Center for Economic and Legal Studies (CRIDE). He is also economic advisor of the European Commission for merger policy. As an economist he is well known from a continuing stream of publications, starting with *L'Enterprise et son Pouvoir de Marché* (1967) Paris: PUF.

H. W. de Jong teaches at the University of Amsterdam. He is the leading Dutch economist in the field of industrial organization. The focus of his scientific work is on the dynamic aspects of economic life. His most important book has been translated into English, under the title *Dynamic Market Theory*. He is also the editor of *The Structure of European Industry* (1989) Deventer: Kluwer.

K. D. George is head of the Department of Economics at University College of Swansea. Together with C. Joll he wrote a well known textbook on industrial organization. George is a member of the UK Monopolies and Mergers Commission. He is internationally recognized as an expert in the field of mergers and merger policy.

E. Kantzenbach is a professor at Hamburg University. In the sixties his dissertation introduced the concept of workable competition in Continental Europe. It stimulated European economists to think about the nature of market competition in relation to economic policy. Later on, Kantzenbach was a longstanding director of the German *Monopolkommission*. Recently he was appointed president of HWWA, *Institut für Wirtschaftsforschung* in Hamburg.

Introduction

This collection of essays results from the F. de Vries Seminar, "Merger control in the EC," held in Rotterdam, in the fall of 1989. Like the audience of the seminar, the reader of this volume is offered a well-balanced presentation of the relevant questions, from authors approaching merger activity from very different angles.

Jacquemin starts from the perspective of European policy, in which market integration is the central tenet. According to studies published by the EC Commission, the potential gains arising from market integration will be spectacular: roughly a 5 percent growth of combined GDP,[1] attributed to the possibility of more efficient re-

---

[1] Emerson, M., assisted by Aujean, M., Catinat, M., Goybet, P., and Jacquemin, A. 1988: The economics of 1992: An assessment of the potential economic effects of completing the internal market of the European Community. *European Economy*, 35.

structuring of industry. Merger activity will play an important role in this process of adaptation to widening markets. It will give rise to greater efficiency in three distinct ways: by allowing greater exploitation of economies of scale and scope; by internalizing activities that involve high transaction costs; and by concentrating activity in the hands of the most able managers.[2]

An open question is how to turn potential gains of mergers into real growth. In this respect it is illuminating to look at empirical research into the effects of merger activity. Several detailed studies have recorded a high failure rate of mergers. This indicates that the benefits are highly uncertain and that merged firms can be confronted with unexpected difficulties. So it would be inadvisable to count the chickens before they are hatched in 1992.

An additional problem is the contribution of mergers to the increase of industrial concentration ratios. There is an implicit danger that merger activity will restrict market competition by creating dominant positions for the combined firms.

Continuing his essay, Jacquemin tries to reconcile failing mergers and threatening market power with the perspective of European policy. For this he selects industries characterized by conditions favorable for merger. Admitting that he does not cover all factors, Jacquemin applies four indicators to distinguish industries according to the expected

---

[2] George, K. (this volume), p. 78.

effects on competition and efficiency. In his view this classification, or a similar one containing more indicators, could be used for a first screening of European merger proposals. If potential merger problems were identified at this stage of a vetting process, the Commission would decide to open proceedings. In the next round, it would have to analyze the effects of the merger on competition by looking at, for instance, the market shares of the firms concerned.

In de Jong's lecture the scene is changed. Instead of the EC integration process, attention focuses on market cycles. Merger activity is described as an adaptation of industries to deteriorating long-term prospects, caused by the downturn of market cycles. According to de Jong, supply and demand curves are constantly shifting up and down, and the degree of industrial concentration is changing all the time. Market conditions flow in such a way that it is not possible to make reliable cost and benefit analyses. The only certain criterion, he argues, is a competitive standard compelling the authorities to block mergers likely to create market dominance at EC level.

A merger policy based on a competitive standard is not enough to guarantee a free market. De Jong argues that national differences in respect to corporate control are causing distortions in international trade, both within the EC, and world-wide. In his view the EC should combine a vigorous competition policy with a free market for corporate control, and in trade with third countries it should insist on reciprocity.

George and Kantzenbach, in contrast with de Jong, try to pinpoint the welfare effects of mergers in their lasting influence on the industrial structure. For the time being, so they argue, causality runs from structure to performance. They stress that structural conditions provide business with the incentives to increase performance unceasingly.

The difference of their approach to Jacquemin's ideas is clearly marked in the screening of merger proposals. George and Kantzenbach are critical of cost–benefit analysis. From experience of merger policy in West Germany, and in Great Britain, they derive the lesson that there is a general tendency to overrate the benefits, and to underrate the costs of mergers. George and Kantzenbach rely on market shares in the first place. In this way they identify what is important in their view: the free market, and with it the competitive pressure to maintain high levels of technical achievement. For Jacquemin, on the other hand, mergers are instrumental to the seizing of opportunities arising from market integration. Therefore he proposes to base decisions in merger policy on a trade-off between the estimated costs and benefits. In doing so he is assuming a more or less transparent process of competition, in which economies of scale are important for efficient production. In my own opinion this means that there is no agreement over the main route of industrial development in the

EC. Market concentration arouses suspicion in the minds of Kantzenbach and George, but for Jacquemin, it is a necessary condition for productive efficiency in a whole series of industries.

The aim of this introduction is to describe how the authors differ in their analysis of merger activity in the EC. It gives only a first impression of important questions which have arisen from the market integration in Europe. We have to admit that industrial economists are unable to provide widely accepted answers. But the discussion has been started; it will give an impulse to theoretical and empirical studies, and maybe we shall witness the development of a coherent European school of thought in the field of industrial organization.

P. H. Admiraal

1

Mergers and European Policy

A. P. JACQUEMIN[1]

---

[1] The views set out in this lecture are expressed in a personal capacity.

1

Introduction

In his de Vries lectures eight years ago, Professor Harold Demsetz neatly expressed the "Chicago approach" to competition. Among other things, he mentioned the professional view of economists active in the foundation of the American Economic Association, and he wrote: "It did not strike them as difficult to justify industrial concentration. They were swept along by the tide of Darwinian thought. Combinations and trusts were regarded as evolutionary social advances, as the outcome of natural laws calling for social cooperation to replace personal actions. They also felt such combinations reflected technological changes calling for larger scale operations."[2] He added: "The

[2] Demsetz, H. 1982: *Economic, legal, and political dimensions of competition.* Amsterdam: North Holland, p. 17.

[3]

United States is now almost two centuries into its unique experiment to strengthen economic competition, however silly that may seem to sociobiologists."[3]

Demsetz's skepticism about a strict anti-trust policy derives from his firm belief in the laissez-faire economic system. Yet, he contends that some competition policies are desirable and, among others, he made the following recommendation: "Consider blocking horizontal mergers only if this keeps an industry from becoming very concentrated, but allow an efficiency defense of such mergers."[4]

It is this view that the famous American humorist, Art Buchwald, pushed to the limit in one of his witty papers, published in the *Washington Post* more than twenty years ago. He imagined the following scenario:

It is 1978 and by this time every company west of the Mississippi will have merged into one giant corporation known as Samson Securities. Every company east of the Mississippi will have merged under an umbrella corporation known as the Delilah Company.

It is inevitable that one day the chairman of the board of Samson and the President of Delilah would meet and discuss merging their two companies ...

... The Anti-Trust Division of the Justice Depart-

[3] Demsetz, 1982, p. 18.
[4] Demsetz, 1982, pp. 53–4.

ment studied the merger for months. Finally the Attorney-General made this ruling:

"While we find some drawbacks to only one company being left in the United States, we feel the advantages to the public far outweigh the disadvantages. Therefore, we're making an exception in this case and allowing Samson and Delilah to merge."

We are in 1989, and clearly there is no danger of monopolization of either the US or the European economies. What we observe, however, is a wave of mergers and acquisitions. In particular, the completion of the European internal market, creating a more integrated demand on a European level, is leading companies to concentrate on their most productive activities, as well as to seek better geographical coverage. One way of achieving these structural adjustments is through merger and acquisition.

The number of transactions between the thousand largest European corporations, rose from 208 in 1984/5, to 383 in 1987/8, and over the period 1984–8 the number of intra-EC transactions almost quadrupled (see table 1.1). As we know, historically, mergers occur in waves; the temptation is to treat each new merger wave as an entirely new phenomenon, requiring new forms of analysis and hypothesis. However, it seems wise to try to link current trends to the basic economic analysis in the field.

In the traditional economics of industrial organ-

Table 1.1 The thousand largest European corporations: mergers and acquisitions of majority holdings 1982–8, by nationality of parties

Year	National (parties from same EC country)	EC (parties from different EC countries)	International (parties from EC + non-EC country)	Total
1982/3	59 (50.5)	38 (32.5)	20 (17.0)	117
1983/4	101 (65.2)	29 (18.7)	25 (16.1)	155
1984/5	146 (70.2)	44 (21.2)	18 (8.7)	208
1985/6	145 (63.7)	52 (23.0)	30 (13.3)	227
1986/7	211 (69.6)	75 (24.8)	17 (5.6)	303
1987/8	214 (55.9)	111 (29.0)	58 (17.8)	383

Figures in brackets represent percentage of overall total.
Source: EC Commission, Report on Competition Policy.

ization, exogenous market structure determines endogenous conduct, and the two jointly determine market performance. By contrast, in the New Industrial Organization analysis, not only is structure endogenous, but the causal relationships between structure, conduct and performance are different: through strategic commitments, conduct may affect structure, either because it has a lasting effect on cost or demand conditions, or because it influences the belief and hence the behavior of rivals, in situations of imperfect information.

Mergers and acquisitions constitute a major example of strategies by which market structure and performance can be modified over time in a more or less irreversible way. They are mainly stimulated by an increased intensity of competitive pressures, induced by phenomena such as an international opportunity, public deregulation, or recession, and the welfare results of these operations are usually multidimensional.

In the first section of this policy paper, the main theoretical arguments concerning the costs and benefits of horizontal mergers as a way of modifying market conditions are identified, and some indicators that could be used to evaluate the probability of these costs and benefits in a European context are explored.

The second section will examine the European merger control proposal, based on the dual view that, while restructuring required by the completion of the European Community's internal market should lead to beneficial concentration of operations in certain areas, simultaneously, these operations may also create harmfully dominant positions.

1 Costs and Benefits of Mergers in the European Context

A sequence of questions can be asked about the effects of horizontal mergers and take-overs. First, what are the theoretical bases for efficiency gains of mergers, and what is the evidence from empirical studies? Secondly, to the extent that there is a net positive contribution to resource productivity, what are the key elements for examining the possible trade-off between the benefits of these mergers and the consequences of enhanced market power?

1.1 Two main types of benefit can be attributed to mergers: a reduction in production and transaction costs, and an improvement in the efficiency of management. But against these potential benefits can also be set possible inefficiencies resulting from mergers.

The role of economies of scale in production is well known. Cost savings can accrue from a better division of labor within the production unit, the spreading of fixed costs, and longer production runs. Mergers which lead to reorganization may help firms to realize these economies, and to attain an optimum scale of efficiency. The scope of the economies achieved will depend on the slope of the average cost curve for output below the optimum level. There can also be scale economies in functions such as transport, distribution and research.

Besides these static scale economies, there is the phenomenon of learning effects associated with increasing experience of production of a good or service. Thus the cost of producing each extra unit decreases as the cumulative output increases.

Finally, mention should be made of the role of "scope economies," whereby the sum of the costs of producing two products separately may be higher than the cost of producing them together. Here, factors such as complementarity are at work. For example, the same indivisible input can be used at once in the production (or distribution) of several goods: by extending its range of products, a firm can thereby reduce its unit costs.

These various phenomena have led many authors[5] to conclude that high concentration – chiefly brought about by mergers – and large market shares are a sign of efficiency, because they show that firms with low costs have increased their market shares at the expense of less efficient firms. The low costs lead in the short run to higher profitability. All these phenomena are thus prompted by the search for efficiency.

But for an organization to benefit from the market, and for such a merger to yield real synergy, machinery within the new entity needs to be set up to make its internal operation efficient. The pitfalls awaiting the large merged organization are legendary: poor communications, sour industrial relations, corporate culture clashes, failure to cut out costly duplication, insufficient coordination, and finally, lack of flexibility.

In recent years, the question of flexibility in an increasingly uncertain world has become more and more important. Some of the difficulties large firms have in adapting to their changing environ-

[5] See, for example, Demsetz, H. 1974: Two systems of belief about monopoly. In Goldschmid, D., Mann, H., and Weston, J. (eds) *Industrial Concentration: The new learning.* Boston: Little Brown; and Peltzman, S. 1977: The gains and losses from industrial organization. *Journal of Law and Economics,* 20.

ment may be due to an over-rigid organization, imposed in the course of increasing concentration. In conditions of great uncertainty about levels of demand, the lesser exploitation of economies of scale by small to medium-sized firms using a flexible technology may be more than offset by their ability to respond to changes in demand. To make a success of a merger, it is necessary to organize the merged unit in such a way as to achieve flexible decentralization.

A second possible benefit of mergers arises from the take-over process. The various forms of take-over can be just as effective a means of transferring control of one company's assets to another as a full legal merger, and the replacement of an acquired company's management can likewise lead to better exploitation of its resources. This "market for corporate control" also reduces the danger of conflicting goals between the owners and managers of companies. To the extent that managers may have different preferences from shareholders, in terms of profits, sales or degree of risk aversion, the take-over mechanism helps reduce the associated distortions. The mere threat of take-over is an incentive for management, or the controlling shareholder, to run a business in the best interests of the company.[6] Conversely, however, many of the defense tactics used against hostile take-overs may be

[6] See Symposium on takeovers. *Journal of Economic Perspective*, 1, winter 1988.

damaging to the interests of the shareholders of the target company, and serve only those of its management. Very strict regulation of take-overs might therefore have undesirable consequences.[7]

One of the basic assumptions behind the favorable view of hostile take-overs is that the stock market correctly reflects the values of the acquired and acquiring firms. This is not necessarily the case, however. The anticipated benefits may not be realized, the take-over failing to improve performance and only redistributing profits from the managers to the owners. Moreover, the management of the predator company may be guided by motives other than profit maximization, motives which reflect other interests, and cause them to pay too high a price for the acquisition. Added to this are various considerations concerning the perverse effects that take-over activity can have on the actual management of companies.

Take-overs may absorb a large proportion of management time and induce some managers to give more attention to financial transactions than to productivity and competitiveness. The threat of take-over encourages the maintenance of excessive liquidity and the pursuit of short-term profit, at the expense of strategic investment that would yield a high return only in the long term. There are

[7] Jarrell, G., Brickley, J., and Netter, J. 1988: The market for corporate control: the empirical evidence since 1980. *Journal of Economic Perspective*, 1.

also dangers for firms taking on increased debt, either to finance or to ward off take-overs. In some cases, key assets needed for an industrial growth or diversification strategy are sold off to finance or prevent a take-over. Finally, frequent changes in the controlling shareholders, decision centers, and headquarters of companies, are apt to affect the ability of management to enter into lasting commitments in relation to specific human capital, and their loyalty to the company.

1.2 The theoretical argument about the contribution of mergers to the productivity of business assets does not yield a general presumption in their favor. It is therefore useful to look at the results of empirical research into the effects of mergers. During the 1960s and 1970s, most mergers in Europe were horizontal, rather than vertical or conglomerate. The little research that has been done in this area found that merger activity considerably increased national industrial concentration ratios.[8] In recent years there has been a new wave of mergers

[8] De Jong, H. 1976: Theory and evidence concerning mergers. In Jacquemin, A. and de Jong, H. (eds) *Markets, corporate behaviour and the State*. The Hague: Nijhoff; Hannah, L. and Kay, J. 1976: *Concentration in modern industry: Theory measurement and the UK experience*. London: Macmillan; Müller, J. 1976: The impact of mergers on concentration: a study of eleven West German industries. *Journal of Industrial Economics*, 25; Ryder, B. 1972: *Mergers in Swedish industry*. Stockholm: Almqvist and Wiksell.

and acquisitions, stimulated partly by the completion of the European internal market, and the majority of these have occurred in already concentrated industries.

As for the effects in terms of profitability and growth, many studies point to the absence of substantial efficiency gains. A comparative study, directed by Mueller,[9] of results from various EC countries concerning full legal mergers concluded that:

1 Tests to identify economies of scale as a possible objective proved it was not significant: for one thing, the size of acquiring firms was usually already greater than the minimum optimum scale for the industry.

2 The tests of post-merger profitability suggested that the mergers had little or no effect on the profitability of the merging firms in the three or five years following the merger; nor was there any significant difference in the returns per share three years after merger. This confirms the results obtained in many American studies.[10]

[9] Mueller, D. 1980: *The determinants and effects of mergers: An international comparison.* Cambridge: Oelgeschlager, Gum and Marin.

[10] Scherer, F. M. 1980: *Industrial market structure and economic performance.* Boston: Houghton Mifflin, 2nd edn, pp. 138–9.

3   It is also suggested that the costs of the changes in organization (difficulty of "digesting" the acquisitions, diseconomies of large organizations) are often greater than the benefits claimed by the promoters of take-overs.

This last point is confirmed by detailed studies of mergers in the UK.[11] Studies by management consultants come to similar conclusions. Coley and Reinton[12] looked at US and British companies in the *Fortune* 250 list and the *Financial Times* 500, which in the past had made acquisitions to enter new markets. They concluded that only 23 percent of the 116 firms analyzed were able to recover the cost of their capital or, better still, the funds invested in the acquisition program. It also appears that the higher the degree of diversification implied by the take-over, the smaller the likelihood of success. For horizontal mergers in which the acquired firm is not large, however, the success rate is around 45 percent. The main reasons for failure appear to be: too high a price paid for the acquisition, over-estimation of the potential of the acquired business in terms of synergy and market

[11]   Cowling, K. et al. 1980: *Mergers and economic performance*. Cambridge University Press; Meeks, G. 1977: *Disappointing marriage: A study of the gains from mergers*. Cambridge University Press.
[12]   Coley, S. and Reinton, S. 1988: The hunt for value. *The McKinsey Quarterly*, spring.

position, and inadequate management of the process of integration after the acquisition. It should be underlined that such a high rate of failure cannot be considered to equate with the normal risks of other business activities. The economic and social consequences of wrong mergers and acquisitions are not simply a question of shareholders' interests, but can affect a large number of stakeholders, employees, as well as local and national economies.

Concerning shareholders, it appears that there is a striking contrast between *ex ante* event studies of corporate mergers' potential gains, and the *ex post* evaluations of the effective results. In his introduction to a recent special article on mergers, Mueller concludes that:

prior to the mergers the shares of acquiring firms tend to outperform the market. At the time of the announcement, there is little change in the acquiring firm's share price. The post-acquisition performance of acquiring company share prices is below their pre-merger performance, and in many studies below that of the market. This post-merger performance matches the constant or declining performance of the acquired units measured in profitability, market shares or productivity. This pattern appears to be characteristic of mergers in Europe and Japan.[13]

[13]   Mueller, D. 1989: Mergers, causes, effects and policies. *International Journal of Industrial Organization, 7.*

1.3   Given these results, one can conclude that, in many cases, there is no real trade-off between efficiency gains from mergers, notably in the form of cost reductions, and an increase in monopoly power, because in the first place net efficiency gains are simply not there. Still, there are situations where the trade-off can be relevant.

A horizontal merger reducing the number of independent firms permits coordinated use of previously independent productive assets (capital, patents, trademarks, etc.) and increases concentration in the relevant market. This increase can lead to higher prices and facilitate collusion.[14] It is then necessary to compare these risks to competition with the potential efficiency gains.

A seminal paper by Williamson[15] proposed a partial equilibrium formula for measuring the respective sizes of cost savings and surplus reductions due to a restriction of output, that a horizontal merger could induce. Williamson suggested that it is sufficient to make a comparison between the "deadweight loss," i.e., the loss of consumer welfare which is not otherwise compensated, and the savings of resources which become available for alternative use.

---

[14]   An illustration of these effects is easily obtained in the case of the Cournot model; see Ordover, J. 1989: *Economic foundations of competition policy.* New York University, mimeo.

[15]   Williamson, O. 1968: Economics as an antitrust defense: The welfare trade-offs. *American Economic Review*, 58.

However, this "naïve" social cost–benefit analysis requires a number of qualifications, including matters of timing and uncertainty, non-price competition, variety of products, x-inefficiency, income distribution effects, and so on.[16] Three aspects are especially relevant in the European context: first, consideration of the new industry structure following mergers; second, the international trade dimension, within the Common Market and with the rest of the world; third, the role of mergers in high technology activities.

Concerning the first aspect, it is necessary to have a model of industrial behavior, explaining the adjustment of prices and quantities in response to a merger. Farrell and Shapiro[17] provide such a model for the Cournot case. A crucial result of their analysis is the role of the response of non-participant firms to any output reduction by the

[16] For a brief review of these aspects, see Jacquemin, A. and Slade, M. 1989: Cartels, collusion and horizontal mergers. In R. Schmalensee and R. Willig (eds) *Handbook of Industrial Organization*. Amsterdam: North Holland. For the case of differentiated products, see Deneckere, R. and Davidson, C. 1985: Incentives to form coalitions with Bertrand competition. *Rand Journal of Economics*, 16. They show that when the merging firms raise their prices, non-participant firms will do the same, since price-reaction schedules slope upward. Mergers will not then increase social welfare.

[17] Farrell, J. and Shapiro, C. 1988: *Horizontal mergers: An equilibrium analysis*. University of California, Berkeley: Program in Law and Economics, working paper, 88-(4).

[17]

merging parties. If non-participant firms reduce their outputs too, the merger may well lower welfare, even though it is profitable. The case is most relevant if the merger makes collusion more likely, or if the oligopolists compete in price among differentiated products,[18] and it becomes more probable the larger the combined market share of the merging firms relative to the (weighted) share of the outsiders. On the contrary, if non-participant firms with large markups expand their outputs noticeably in response to the merger, a significant welfare gain can be provided.[19]

In the European market context, this leads to the consideration of several phenomena.[20] The suppression of non-tariff barriers, by making easier arbitrage for buyers and intermediaries, leads to an expanding market and a larger potential demand, so that there is a high probability that firms not participating in a merger will be very responsive to price increases, and will tend to expand their outputs. This conjecture is reinforced in expanding

---

[18] Indeed the merger permits the two combined price-competing firms to raise their price and induce non-participant firms to raise the price of competing substitutes.

[19] Let us recall that in a Cournot equilibrium, large markups are associated with large market shares, and large firms have lower marginal costs.

[20] For several of these aspects, see Jacquemin, A., Buigues, P., and Ilzkovitz, F. 1989: Horizontal mergers and competition policy in the European Community. *European Economy*, 40.

industries, given that a growing market attracts many entries; these entries are relatively easy, because incumbent firms have fewer advantages in terms of cost, experience, and reputation, than when established in mature or declining industries. Furthermore, many mergers and take-overs in the EC conform to a twofold strategy: firms acquire assets in the activities they are best at, and sell assets related to activities in which their competitive position is weak; and they extend their geographical sphere of operation by buying up firms in other member states in their core business. This trend, according to which firms prefer to concentrate on their top-grade products, and increase their geographical diversification, as an alternative to product diversification in a limited geographical area, is compatible with an industry structure favorable to output expansion.[21] Finally, even a reduction in total output induced by the merger could be compatible with an increase in social welfare if the redistribution of output among firms were to lead to sufficient cost savings. This possibility is in line with the Smith and Venables model[22] applied to European integration: the lowering of non-tariff barriers could produce a net

[21] Buigues, P. and Jacquemin, A. 1989: Strategies of firms and structural environments in the large internal market. *Journal of Common Market Studies*, May.
[22] Smith, A. and Venables, A. 1988: Completing the internal market in the European Community. *European Economic Review*, 32.

gain in social welfare even if the number of firms were to decrease, because the smaller consumer surplus associated with increased concentration would be more than offset by the improvement in returns to producers, due to exploitation of economies of scale. Previously mentioned empirical studies indicate, however, that this is far from being a general case and that we must not overstate the incidence and importance of scale economies in the total population of industries.

At the same time, existing data suggest that the total number of mergers and acquisitions involving at least one of the top thousand EC firms has been steadily increasing, from 155 in 1983/4 to 383 in 1987/8. Seventy percent of mergers in 1987/8, compared with 50 percent in 1984/5, involved firms, from among these top thousand, with sales of over ECU[23] 1 billion. This trend may be dangerous to the extent that positive welfare effects are less probable if the market share of the merging firms is large relative to that of the non-participant firms, and to the extent that the more power the merging firms hold pre-merger, the larger the cost reduction must be in order for the post-merger price to fall.

The international dimension is another crucial factor for evaluating the impact of European mergers. It is well known that competition from imports considerably limits the market power of

[23]   European currency units.

[20]

domestic producers. A recent econometric study,[24] using a sample of over one hundred three-digit European manufacturing sectors, confirms that imports from intra- and extra-EC origins exert a significant disciplinary effect on price-cost margins, but with a greater impact played by extra-EC imports. The pressure of potential imports, held back by existing trade barriers, as well as actual import competition, has a significant impact. All other things being equal, it is therefore probable that mergers in industries which are relatively open to international trade, from within or outside the Community, are less dangerous for competition than mergers in relatively closed industries.

This presumption has been analyzed in a series of recent studies. Ross,[25] for instance, shows that the lowering of tariff barriers is more effective in limiting the price-increasing effects of a merger, the greater the number of foreign firms. However, foreign competition is far from being a perfect substitute for domestic competition, in that it is subject to extra uncertainties that do not affect domestic production. Ordover and Willig[26] have

[24] Jacquemin, A. and Sapir, A. 1989: The discipline of imports in the European market: An econometric analysis. *CPER* working paper.
[25] Ross, T. 1988: On the price effects of mergers in the freer trade. *International Journal of Industrial Organization*, 2.
[26] Ordover, J. and Willig, R. 1988: *Perspectives on mergers and world competition*. Princeton: discussion paper, 88.

put forward a model which suggests that the effectiveness of competition policy depends on the protectionism of trade policy, via tariffs and quotas. Macroeconomic policy also plays a role: the effect of a reduction in the number of domestic producers is very sensitive not only to the number of foreign firms, but also to the level and variability of the exchange rate. If the main protection against domestic monopoly power is imports, exchange rate volatility will lessen this protection. From this point of view, the European Monetary System could indirectly have a beneficial impact on competition in the Common Market.

An inverse problem is the monopoly power effect of EC mergers on the rest of the world. If we assume a selfish policy of maximizing domestic social welfare and ignoring the perverse effects on the rest of the world, the only losses that need be considered by a European merger policy are the reductions in the European consumer surplus, and the only gains the increase in the profits of European producers. All things being equal, the net European gain in welfare resulting from a merger would be greater, the larger the degree of European involvement in the merger, and lower, the greater the proportion of the output consumed in Europe.

A third aspect especially relevant in the European context is the role of mergers in high technology industries. Over recent years, the Community has lost world market shares in several of these sectors (for instance, electrical and electronic equipment, information technology ...). These industries are highly R & D intensive. Because of the indivisibilities in R & D up to certain thresholds, and because firms require a sufficient scale of operation in order to undertake research programs, and for many other economic reasons, linkups between European firms in such industries are justified. They increase the resources available, and so encourage the undertaking of more ambitious (and risky) projects which single firms cannot afford. Mergers in this field also help cut out duplication, and may encourage transfers of technology, thus speeding up the process of innovation. Ordover and Baumol, in their analysis of mergers in high technology industries, conclude:

mergers in high technology industries, in which technologies and products are short-lived, should raise fewer concerns than would similar mergers in industries which have entered their stable phase. This suggestion holds as long as high-technology mergers do not combine firms with large shares of substitute R & D assets that also require large shares of market specific assets for their effective exploitation.[27]

[27] Ordover, J. and Baumol, W. 1988: Antitrust policy and high technology industries. *Oxford Review of Economic Policy*, 4, 32.

On the whole, the message here is that when there is a trade-off between static and dynamic efficiency, it is wise to favor the long-run dynamic performance that is expected to ultimately overcome any static loss. Still, the existence of such a trade-off can be questioned in most industries. In fact, evidence suggests that R & D is not characterized by substantial economies of scale, and that monopoly power can be expected to inhibit R & D and technological advance in the long run.[28] Furthermore, avoiding wasteful duplication, internalizing external effects, and insuring a large dissemination of knowledge, might all be achieved through other, less dangerous devices than full merger, such as R & D cooperation at the "precompetitive stage."[29] At best, what can be argued is that in industries characterized by short-lived high technology and rapidly expanding demand, all other things being equal, the prospect of efficiency gains is enhanced and the danger of monopoly power is limited. In the European context, how-

[28] Neumann, M., Böbel, I., and Haid, A. 1982: Innovation and market structure in West German industries. *Managerial and Decision Economics*, 3. See also Geroski, P. 1987: *Competition and innovation*. Brussels: report prepared for the EC Commission.
[29] Katz, M. 1986: An analysis of cooperative research and development. *Rand Journal of Economics*, winter; D'Aspremont, C. and Jacquemin, A. 1988: Cooperative and non-cooperative R & D in duopoly with spillovers. *American Economic Review*, 5.

[24]

ever, we can observe that the rapid rise in the number of mergers and acquisitions involving firms in the top thousand has been less rapid in the high-growth, high technology sectors than in the rest of industry.

On the basis of the previous discussion, it is tempting to use some basic criteria to classify industries on a prima facie basis, according to the expected effects on competition and efficiency. An illustration of this approach is given in table 1.2, elaborated for a first screening of European merger proposals. Four indicators, from among many others, have been used: prospects of efficiency gains are based on the relative importance of economies of scale and of technological content; dangers of reduced competition rely on the degree of trade openness and the growth rate of market demand.[30]

2 European Policy on Mergers

2.1 There is no article in the Treaty of Rome which specifically deals with mergers and acquisitions. However, both the Commission and the

---

[30] An application of this type of classification to the 120 European manufacturing industries at the three-digit NACE level has been made in Jacquemin, Buigues, and Ilzkovitz, 1989.

[25]

Table 1.2 Illustration of an industrial classification according to the expected effects on competition and efficiency of a merger

| | | Prospects of efficiency gains (scale economies and technological content) | |
		Weak	Strong
Danger of reduction of competition (degree of trade openness and growth rate of demand)	Strong	examples: – tobacco products – metal goods	examples: – electrical plant and machinery – railway rolling stock
	Weak	examples: – textiles and clothing – leather goods	examples: – telecommunications – computers

European Court of Justice have interpreted Articles 85 and 86, the two pillars of EC competition policy, in such a way as to make them partly applicable to mergers.

[26]

Article 86 prohibits the abuse of a dominant position. The "dominant position" referred to in this Article relates to "a position of economic strength enjoyed by an undertaking which enables it to prevent effective competition being maintained on the relevant market by giving it the power to behave, to an appreciable extent, independently of its competitors, customers and ultimately of its consumers" (decision of the European Court of Justice in the *United Brands* case, 1978).

Clearly, many factors are relevant when establishing the existence of dominance. In their decisions, the Commission and the Court commonly look to market shares and barriers to entry. This implies the determination of the product and relevant geographical market, taking into account factors such as product differentiation and import penetration, and identification of the conditions of entry, based on supply and demand substitutability, existing contracting practices, and producer information exchanges. On the other hand, and in contrast with the US approach, there is almost no use of numerical guidelines, such as a certain change in the Herfindhal index or the ability, after the merger, to raise prices by some fixed percentage above existing levels. The European approach is simultaneously more comprehensive and more pragmatic; in the light of recent theoretical literature, this is probably for the best.

It is not illegal to achieve a dominant position:

[27]

only the abusive exploitation of such a position is prohibited. Some examples of such abuses are given in Article 86 itself: the imposition of inequitable prices, the restriction of output, discrimination, and tying clauses. These practices correspond to a possible direct misuse of dominance which damages consumers' interests.[31] But a broader conception of an abuse could take into account not only the direct impact of market conduct on market performance, but also the indirect effect, through the loop going from market conduct to market structure. In this view, Article 86 could be used to attack business strategies which modify, in a more or less irreversible way, the conditions of supply and demand in such a way that, in the end, social welfare is harmed.

This is the line of reasoning followed by the Commission and the Court. In the *Continental Can* case (1973), where Continental Can took control of the leading Benelux producer of metal cans through its wholly-owned Belgian subsidiary, the Court found that since the concept of abuse is not defined more precisely in Article 86, the Community's objectives set out in the Treaty of Rome must be considered before the examples of abuse given

---

[31] Business practices are usually not obviously abusive, and even those mentioned in Article 86 could be not only compatible with competition, but may actually enhance it, in a general context of imperfect competition. This can be the case with price discrimination and non-linear pricing.

[28]

in Article 86 itself. An abuse was held to be present where an enterprise conducts itself in a way that is "objectively" wrong in relation to the goals of the Treaty:

[the] provision is not only aimed at practices which may cause damage to consumers directly, but also at those which are detrimental to them through their impact on an effective competition structure, such as is mentioned in Article 3(f) of the Treaty. Abuse may therefore occur if an undertaking in a dominant position strengthens such a position in such a way that the degree of dominance reached substantially fetters competition, i.e., that only undertakings remain in the market whose behaviour depends on the dominant one.

Thus the Commission considers that the market structure as such has to be protected: a change in the supply structure which virtually eliminates the alternative sources of supply to the consumer appears to be an abuse in itself. Although the Court annulled the Commission's decision in the *Continental Can* case – mainly because the relevant market was not adequately defined – it very clearly confirmed the soundness of its interpretation: Article 86 may be applied to mergers.[32]

[32] Ambiguities remain, however. According to the Court, it can be considered an abuse if an enterprise extends a dominant position to the point where the objectives of the Treaty are threatened through a substantial alteration of the supply

[29]

More recently the relevance of Article 85 for merger policy has also been established. This Article condemns agreements between firms which may affect competition within the Common Market. In the *Philip Morris* case (1987), the Court decided that agreements on the acquisition of a minority shareholding in a competitor may come within the ambit of Article 85.[33] This would be the case, the Court considered, especially where, by acquisition of a shareholding or additional clauses in the agreement, the investing company gained legal or actual control over the commercial behavior of the other company. The Court also stressed that conduct does not cease to be anti-competitive merely by reference to the legal form in which it is presented.

Although through these two judgments the Commission has obtained power to control acquisitions and mergers, this power is still limited, and not very effective. With Article 86, the control only concerns firms which are already dominant,

---

situation, so that the consumer's freedom of action in the market is seriously jeopardized. Hence, to be condemned, the extension must amount to a substantial alteration of the market structure. This implies that the distinction between the creation of a dominant position and its abuse becomes very doubtful.

[33] The case concerned an agreement under which Philip Morris acquired a 30.8 percent shareholding in its competitor Rothmans International.

and in principle is made after merger or acquisition has occurred. The economic, financial, and social costs of an eventual dismemberment after the operation has been fulfilled would be generally prohibitive, however; furthermore the absence of clear rules in terms of competence and procedures creates legal uncertainty for firms, including possible conflicts of jurisdiction. Article 85 has a very limited domain of application, as it requires the existence of an agreement and excludes cases of full control. This explains why the Commission proposed, as far back as in 1973, a specific regulation on Community merger control. In the 1992 perspective, and given the corresponding wave of mergers and take-overs, it is happy that such a regulation has been adopted.

The new text elaborated in 1989 is founded upon two main points,[34] each of which corresponds to delicate economic problems:

1 The regime creating a mandatory prior notification is applicable to major mergers which have a truly European dimension, linked to trans-

[34] A third important aspect is to provide legal certainty for firms subject to the controls. This requires that the Commission and the Court have exclusive jurisdiction over mergers of a Community dimension ("one-stop shop") in order to avoid conflicts of jurisdiction and a clear procedure leading to decisions within tight deadlines. For an analysis of these questions, see Jacquemin, Buigues, and Ilzkovitz, 1989.

[31]

national externalities. The aim is to prevent both the creation and the enlargement of dominant market positions.

2 The regulation apparently does not provide for authorization in derogation from the prohibition, on the basis of the efficiency effects of the merger.

2.2 In the Commission's Regulation, the first two articles state that the mergers covered by the Regulation are those which have a Community dimension; among them, mergers which create or strengthen a dominant position in the Common Market, or a substantial part of it, are to be condemned. As far as the definition of a "Community dimension" of operation is concerned, a criterion based on turnover is used. In the initial phase of enforcement, a merger operation is considered to be of a Community dimension, and thus subject to regulation when the total world-wide turnover of the total number of firms concerned represents a sum in excess of ECU 5 billion, and the total turnover realized within the Community by at least two of the firms involved represents a figure in excess of ECU 250 million. It is not, however, considered to be an operation with a Community dimension if each one of the firms concerned realizes two-thirds of its total Community turnover within one and the same member state.

Recourse to such thresholds is guided by a concern to achieve the minimum level of legal uncertainty relating to the scope of the ruling, since the calculation of turnover is much more direct than that of market shares, and by the desire to limit to an operational level the number of cases to be examined. Whatever the precise numerical value of the thresholds, this choice of parameter calls for important caveats. First, the use of firm size is clearly suspect, both on economic and legal grounds. Size has indeed to be viewed within the context of the relevant market. Secondly, even for sectors aggregated at a three-digit level, this threshold is sometimes quite high in relation to the amount of economic activity concerned, so that a complete monopolization could fall beyond the scope of application; for other sectors the figure is low when compared with the total value of Community production.

Among the criteria which assist the process of deciding whether or not there exists the creation, or the reinforcement, of a dominant position are the following:

- market position, and economic and financial power of the firms concerned;
- the possibility of choosing suppliers and consumers;
- access to supplies or to markets;

- the structure of the markets affected, taking into account international competition;
- barriers to entry (legal or *de facto*);
- supply and demand trends for the goods or services concerned;
- technical and economic progress.

It is to be noted that there is no reference to the existing degree of concentration. Some other criteria are mentioned, such as "market position," "economic and financial power of the firms concerned," and "structure of the markets affected." These factors are at best ambiguous indicators, without clear economic content. Market position, for example, can only be determined by reference to a number of structural features. Market structure itself encompasses the distribution of market shares and entry barriers, which are mentioned separately. As for economic and financial power, this probably cannot be equated with a size or peformance criterion, since the Court of Justice has explicitly rejected the relevance of these two factors for establishing the existence of a dominant position.

That leaves five criteria: The "possibilities of choice of suppliers and consumers" are key elements in market definition. "Access to supplies or markets" is related to vertical integration, but is an important factor in the identification of entry barriers. These are explicitly mentioned under the

[34]

heading "the existence of legal or *de facto* barriers to entry." The same applies to "international competition," which must be taken into account in defining the relevant market, in measuring market shares and in evaluating entry barriers. Finally, a dynamic aspect is taken into account in the reference to the "trend of supply and demand for the goods or services concerned" and to "technical and economic progress." As we have seen, such trends can lead to a presumption of greater or lesser competitive pressure.

The overall impression is that the list of criteria for identifying the creation or the reinforcement of a dominant position is unsystematic, and needs to be fleshed out by guidelines elucidating their content and their use.

2.3 As seen in the previous section, some efficiency gains can be expected from mergers, especially in the context of the restructuring required for the achievement of the internal market. On the other hand, empirical evidence from past experience does not justify a general presumption in favor of mergers as a very effective way of achieving the objective of improved productivity of business assets. It is in this context that the approach adopted in the Regulation must be considered.

The apparent rule is that an operation which creates or reinforces a dominant position is not acceptable even if the negative effects on competition are more than compensated for by the positive

[35]

economic effects. This holds true if the merger contributes to improving technical or economic progress. Indeed, technical and economic progress can be taken into account for identifying the creation or the reinforcement of a dominant position, but only if such a progress benefits the consumers and *is not an obstacle to competition*. Therefore the use of such a criterion cannot be a basis for a derogation to the interdiction of creating or reinforcing a dominant position. If the text is strictly applied, this implies that European competition policy towards mergers and acquisitions is stricter than most other national legislations.

Conclusion

The 1992 program marks a new stage in the European competitive environment, and is leading to new challenges for corporate strategies. The observed restructuring taking place is being made through internal and external operations that differ substantially among industries, leading to relocation and geographical expansion, new product line selections, better exploitation of scale and scope economies, coordination and concentration of dispersed activities. Mergers and take-overs are one of the possible routes of such a restructuring.

The first section of this paper has discussed

theoretical arguments and the results of empirical studies intended to determine the ability of these operations to improve the productivity of business assets in the new context. The main conclusion is that although mergers and take-overs can indeed lead to cost savings and efficiency gains, neither theory nor empirical work provides any cast-iron arguments in favor of a presumption that these operations are generally efficient. Furthermore, even when they are efficient, the corresponding gains must be compared with the effects of a possible increase in monopoly power. This leads to complex trade-offs where the expected new industry structure following the merger, the degree of openness to international trade, and the long-run dynamic performance linked with learning and technical change, are especially relevant aspects in the European context. Such complexity suggests that it would be presumptuous to advocate fine-tuned optimal merger policy.

The second section has shown that a worthwhile, pragmatic approach has been adopted in both the application of Article 85 and 86 of the Rome Treaty to mergers, as well as in the new Regulation creating a prior notification of concentrations having a Community dimension. But this lecture has also shown that at least two aspects require further investigation.

First, the main criteria for identifying the creation, or the strengthening, of a dominant position, such as market shares, conditions of entry, international openness, effects on global output, intensity of technology, and conduct of firms in the relevant market, must be made more explicit in future guidelines.

Second, the official absence of an "efficiency" defense could lead to surreptitious forms of interventions and to internal compromises in the implementation of the Regulation. Indeed, it is not clear that such a strict position will be sustainable in the future.

2

Mergers and Competition Policies: Some General Remarks

H. W. DE JONG

2

1 The Merger Scenery

During the past century there have been four merger waves: around the turn of the century; in the
aftermath of the First World War and during the
twenties; since the late fifties, and especially during
the second half of the sixties, rising to a peak in the
period 1968–73; and, finally, during the eighties,
following the end of the deep recession of the
years 1979–82. Each of these merger waves was of
an intercontinental nature, occurring simultaneously – albeit with differing intensities – in the major
economies of the economically relevant world. In
the present, fourth wave, for example, firms from
European countries and from the United States are
active in restructuring themselves and their markets; likewise, Australian, Canadian, Japanese,
Korean, Kuwaiti and South African companies are
taking part in the world-wide merger and divestment activity.

It is noteworthy that these periods of hectic merger activity (1890–1905, 1918–29, 1958–73, 1983 onwards), were characterized by two significant features. First, a higher than average rate of growth, and a higher than average level of the share of international trade in the gross domestic products of the Western world economies, increasing the competitive pressure on firms. For example, the share of international trade in the world's GDP (in what we now call the OECD area) had reached the unprecedented level of 15 percent in 1899; it fell sharply in the following decades, under the influence of military conflicts, regaining a level of 12 percent in 1929, after which it declined and stagnated, until it rose again around 1960 (to 9 percent), and soared until 1970 (13 percent). Trade growth stagnated after the 1974 oil crisis, but the 1980s saw the resumption of faster rate of growth in world trade, both in merchandise and in services, than in world output. The GATT has just released figures which show a higher rate of growth for trade than for output in every year since 1983. Manufactures, capital goods and services have increased particularly strongly; manufactures account for more than 70 percent of merchandise trade, against a figure of 55 percent at the beginning of the decade. The expansion of trade in services has outstripped even the growth of merchandise exports, and now stands at slightly less than 20 percent of total trade in goods and services of both developed and developing countries.[1] Thus, world trade is again the engine of world economic growth; at the same time, it is an engine that spreads the virus of more intensive competition.

Secondly, the periods of rapid trade growth were also eras of relative price stability: during the four periods of merger activity mentioned earlier, the five-year moving average of the consumer price level deviated by not more than 5 percent from the average in the OECD area. In contrast, other periods (the thirties, forties, and the seventies, for example) were characterized by sharply inflationary or deflationary tendencies. Thus, it can be established that rapid trade growth, more intense competition, relative price stability, and intercontinental merger waves, occurred together.

Is this more than a simple or haphazard concurrence? To my mind, it is; the causality cannot be otherwise construed than fast trade growth and more intense (international) competition spurring on mergers. In each of the four periods of hectic merger activity, it was the pressure of enhanced national and international competition, reflecting the rise of buyers' markets, decreasing transport and communication costs, technological progress

---

[1] *Financial Times*, 15 September, 1989.

[43]

and the international spread of companies, which led to the efforts to restructure the organization of firms and markets. The urge to merge is fed by the need to compete. So much for the general explanation of the recurring merger movements.

2 The Competitive Cycle

Most industries go through market or competitive cycles, as the firms constituting those industries innovate and expand, organize output and distribution, and cope with the uncertainties peculiar to their trades. Success in performing those functions finds its reward in the creation of surplus value, or net economic profit. At the same time, it draws imitative and emulative reactions from established competitors, newcomers, and from companies in other trades or countries who integrate and diversify into the expanding markets. In such a succession of events it is practically impossible to keep a balance between supply and demand. In due course, market creation, resulting in demand running ahead of supply and giving rise to shortages, lengthening delivery times, and price increases (the sellers' market) becomes the obverse: supply overtakes demand, overcapacities arise, and prices decline (a buyers' market).[2] Structural adaptations become imperative: by means of cartels, mergers, or take-overs, firms try to stabilize their relationships. (Dropouts and internal reorganizations obviously occur also, but do not interest us here.)

Such market cycles are industry-specific; that is, the swings have industry-specific amplitudes and periodicities, based on a distinctive course of events. As a rule, the cycle's impact is more pronounced the more capital intensive the industry. Still more generally, it may be said that the flexibility of response of supply to market expansion is decisive. Entry is important, but so is the feasibility of an extension of supply by established producers.

When the market cycle moves from a sellers' to a buyers' market, firms experience an increasing intensity of competition, and prices are pressed downward. The prospects for profits are dimmed, expansion plans are shelved, and overcapacity looms as a threat, or becomes a reality the longer the downturn lasts. Competition, formerly rivalry for expansion, becomes a contest for survival.

In such conditions, firms will seek to cooperate,

---

[2] In a static market model, sellers' and buyers' markets may be defined with reference to a given price at a particular moment; in a dynamic view of the market process, these terms express a succession of moments at which the unba-

or they may try to merge and bid for competitors. If long-term prospects worsen, they may withdraw from the industry, or try to diversify. Structural adjustments are therefore a reaction to changing competitive pressures, but, naturally, some firms (mainly the stronger or more entrepreneurial ones) make a virtue of necessity, strategically positioning themselves in an offensive stance in case the cycle revives. The restructuring of industries is therefore simultaneously both a defensive and an offensive affair, a reaction to preceding events and an anticipation of future developments. However, the turmoil accompanying the market cycle's course usually increases the uncertainties and confusions to such an extent that rational decisions become difficult to take. Many errors, based on misjudgments, creep in, contributing to relative shifts of market shares and profitability. In some cases, exceptional organizers may seize the opportunity to establish a dominant firm with a long-term commanding monopoly position (J. D. Rockefeller's Standard Oil Trust, E. Kirdorf's Rhinish-Westfalian Coal Syndicate, and H. Oppenheimer's De Beer's Diamond Group, provide some prominent examples of this happening).

In most industries, a new upturn of market

---

lanced market situation prevails. Also buyers' markets may occur temporarily in fast-growing industries and sellers' markets in stagnating or declining industries, though, more usually, it is the other way round.

cycles will take care of the preceding restructurings, in the sense that these will be subjected to the discipline of renewed competition, based on improvements, innovations and cost reductions. But society does need an effective competition policy to prevent or remedy the creation of the more dominant positions, evolving within rigid market structures. Competition or merger policy is therefore basically a corrective, needed to keep the market process intact as an open free system.

The reality of market cycles can only be demonstrated for each separate industry, and its sub-sectors, which are to be defined, as the US Supreme Court once held, as "the areas of competition," i.e., composed of those firms which rival each other. But whether it be airlines, petrochemicals, heavy electrical machinery, computers, insurance, textiles or food and drink retailing, these industries all exhibit market cycles, which can be traced by individual studies. The crucial question is whether intensified competition in the declining or stagnating part of the cycle gives rise to cartels and mergers or take-overs, such as to be clearly distinguishable from the other parts of the cycle. Table 2.1 gives a survey of the world oil industry's experience over the past hundred years. It will be seen that rising oil cycles have been accompanied by hardly any restructuring; by contrast, declining cycles, characterized by sharp competition or the prospect thereof, have been accompanied by heavy merger movements, fre-

Table 2.1 Market cycles and mergers/cartels in the oil industry

Period	Price trend	Restructurings
1872–90	declining	Cartel struggles and take-overs leading up to the formation of the Standard Oil Trust (1882)
1890–1900	rising	–
1900–10	declining	1900/1 Discovery of spindle top and formation of Texan oil companies. Anti-trust action against Standard Oil; formation of Asiatic Petroleum (1902) and Royal Dutch-Shell (1907)
1910–20	rising	Break-up of Standard Oil (1911)
1926–35/6	declining	Redline and Achnacarry Agreements (1928) and many mergers, e.g., amongst successors of the Standard Oil Company. Formation of Mobil Oil and Caltex
1936–48	rising	Occasional mergers in the US (1940/1)

1949–52/3	declining	Mergers throughout the period. Formation of Pennzoil and Amoco, and Aramco
1954–8	rising	Few take-overs (in Europe: Regent Oil by Texaco)
1958–70	declining	Many mergers in the US and Europe (e.g., Texaco); formation of OPEC (1960–2)
1970–80	rising	OPEC cartel raises prices in 1973 and 1979
1980/1–present	declining	Spate of mergers and take-over bids. Breakdown of OPEC

Sources: Hamilton, A. 1986: *Oil, the price of power*, p. 9, records annual crude oil prices between 1860 and 1973; Linde, C. van der, 1990 (forthcoming): *Market conditions, development and structure of the international oil industry*, charts crude oil prices between 1860 and 1985.

quent take-over bids, and the formation of cartel agreements and industry trusts. As for the most recent turnaround, both world production and consumption moved downward in 1978/9, with market prices following soon, and posted OPEC prices only in 1982/3. The major oil acquisitions starting in 1979 were undertaken in the turmoil of a reversing market, for reasons given in Davidson's

[49]

exposé of those years.[3] With hindsight, several of those reasons appear questionable, however.

In a more general context, I have demonstrated that stagnating or declining sectors in US and West German industry show rising concentration.[4] Likewise, Uekusa demonstrated the same tendency for Japanese industry.[5] K. D. George stressed that businesses have some "acceptable balance between safety and competition," which may be upset by drastic changes in the environment. Mergers are then a mechanism to restore this.[6]

3 Partial Explanations

The competitive cycle theory disposes of a number of partial explanations:

• Mergers and take-overs are not generally the result of whimsical inclinations of business leaders, nor do they – save for some exceptions

[3] Brooks, J. 1987: *The Takeover Game*. New York: pp. 178–9. Davidson, K. M. 1985: *Megamergers*. Cambridge (Mass.): chapter 12.

[4] On market theory. In Dankbaar, B., Groenewegen, J., and Schenk, H. (eds) 1990: *Perspectives on industrial organization*. Dordrecht/Boston: Kluwer.

[5] Uekusa, 1987: Industrial organization: the 1970s to the present. In Yamamura, K. and Yasuba, Y. (eds) *The political economy of Japan*. Vol. 1, Stanford: p. 484.

[6] George, K. D. and Joll, C. 1981: *Industrial organization*. London: George Allen & Unwin (3rd edn), pp. 74–5.

– represent speculative activities. Even though such phenomena may occur in a number of cases, the implied arguments cannot explain the thousands of mergers and take-overs occurring each year in various sectors of widely differing national economies throughout several continents. If one is prepared to admit some measure of irrationality and speculative moods within the economic system, that nevertheless rules out confusion as a universal principle: "there is reason in madness" (Shakespeare).

- The same holds true for stock market explanations: mergers have been important in countries both with and without developed stock markets, and in fact, in all countries the majority of mergers do not occur on the stock exchange.

- Institutional explanations, such as fiscal changes, the sharpening of cartel laws or employee stock option plans likewise fall through: they lack the generality of a cause that accounts for world-wide movements. But it is true that institutional causes may change the forms of the combination movement in a particular country.

- Neither market power, nor efficiency or size-oriented explanations are of more than partial value. If Chicago-inspired economists maintain that mergers are undertaken for efficiency reasons, the question they are then faced with is why mergers are not undertaken in certain periods when efficiency is obviously of paramount importance, e.g., the thirties or the fifties? And if the managerial striving for size were decisive, it would be difficult to make clear why such strivings are largely absent in some periods, e.g., the fifties or during the eighties, when the quest for value creation, slimming off, and returning to the core business have been setting the scenery.

Why is the search for a tenable, general explanation of merger movements so important? There may be two reasons.

First, the number of partial explanations is nearly endless, and their invocation would require a specification of their relative weights in order to determine their importance. Only important reasons for mergers and take-overs would qualify as goals of merger policy, otherwise such policy would be directed towards temporary, or trifling phenomena. Now, it has turned out to be next to impossible to establish the relative values of partial explanations, which also have a habit of changing with the times.

Secondly, it is not for nothing that anti-trust policies, having as their general goals such criteria as the general interest, or size as such, or consumer welfare, or the achievement of optimal market structure, have generally not made much impact. For one thing, the pace with which markets change is too fast for government regulations to keep up with. For example, within ten years of deregulation of the US airline industry, we have seen the development of intensive competition, followed by mergers and concentration in a "big five" group; more recently there has been the European assault on several of these leading companies, which was only stopped by an administrative decision. Clearly, anti-trust policy could not have devised and applied an optimal size or market structure criterion in time to prevent these events, even supposing such an exercise would have been worth-while. For another, competition policy, and especially merger policy, is always caught in the crossfire of the interest groups concerned, and vague criteria, such as the public interest or consumer welfare, leave wide discretion to the authorities concerned, either to do nothing at all (as in the Netherlands), or to promote national champions (as in France), or – in case important precedents are set – to reverse them (as in the West German Daimler–Benz affair, and the Guinness case).

4 Implications for EC Competition Policy

For these, and other reasons, the establishment of a general standard requiring the protection of the competitive process as the single and unique goal of competition policy is both the most desirable and the most fitting rule. For, if mergers are generally inspired by the seizing of opportunities to try to beat the competition, as was outlined above, a number of mergers (albeit a minority) could make a virtue out of necessity, by establishing dominant positions or monopolies: monopoly, or dominance, is the reward of this dialectical process, and even if only temporary, can exact heavy tolls in terms of loss of welfare and rigidity.

Statutes such as the Sherman Act or the Treaty of Rome (Articles 85 and 86), by compelling the authorities to wield the competitive standard in cartel and merger policies, offer the best guarantee that the free market process is kept intact. And, whereas it may perhaps be regretted that the framers of the Common Market Treaty did not incorporate a specific merger control article, the fact remains that the EC Commission already has the power to block mergers which extend dominance, or establish dominance, which would be hard to contest. The latter point may be greeted skeptically by a number of lawyers, who stipulate that Article 86 requires the existence of dominance before the act of merger. But this is only of theoretical importance, because nearly all cases – even the smaller ones, such as the *Amicon–Fortia/Wright* case of 1981 – involve existing dominance, if not at the EC market level, then in at least a substantial part of the EC market, such as a national state or a part thereof. Moreover, the market has its own way of dealing with sectorally or regionally limited dominance positions, as the *Berisford–Napier* case (1983) demonstrated: the Commission stopped the investigation because a number of customers had transferred their purchases to other suppliers. And finally, a merger creating dominance at the EC level, say between Volkswagen and Fiat, which would establish a market leader with more than a 30 percent market share in motor cars, might well be challenged, even if it remains below the current standard of 40 percent. For, already in the Tenth CPR of 1980 (no. 150) the Commission has wisely let it be known that it might be able to challenge mergers creating a market share position between 20 percent and 40 percent. The criterion is competition, not size as such.

It is said that the existing Article 86 regime is imperfect in a number of respects:

- It was never drafted as a merger instrument. But as long as it can be used efficiently, so what?
- It creates no duty to give advance notice of mergers. So let the Commission make it be widely known that relevant cases (falling within guidelines) will be dealt with swiftly; also, advance notification could be build into the present system.
- It is said to provide no time limits. Is this something the Commission should necessarily correct? In some cases (Berisford, for example)

it can now take a year to investigate them, instead of the few months allowed in the merger proposal.

- It does not allow for exemption under regional or technological policies. But this is not regretted by the many who would fear the introduction of so-called industrial policies, which have a habit of confusing competition policy issues, under the pressure of vested interests.

- It is said that the Common Market law addresses itself only to single-firm dominance, and not to threats resulting from the creation of joint market power, for example through oligopoly behavior.[7] However, oligopoly as a structural feature is difficult to define precisely, and it depends on circumstances (internal cohesion, entry barriers, market growth, international competition, technological progress, etc.) as to whether an "oligopoly" has joint market power or not, and to what degree. Moreover, within the EC, concerted behavior of firms can be dealt with under Article 85; and also bids which involve groups of firms (e.g., the *Irish Distillers Group* case of May 1988).

At the time of writing, discussion about the merger proposals put forward by the Commission

[7] Fox, E. M. 1986: Monopolization and dominance in the United States and the European Community: Efficiency, opportunity and fairness. *Notre Dame Law Review*, 6, 5, 989–90.

still continues. But reports coming from Brussels
inspire some optimism: even though the minimum
size of merger in which the Commission may in-
tervene (ECU 5 billion, or ECU 2 billion, or something in between) is still a moot point, the competitive
guideline as the only criterion for clearing important mergers seems agreed upon. Furthermore, the
important principle of exclusive one-stop control
by the Commission is secured by the rule that a
merger cleared by the Commission can only be re-
examined by the authorities in a particular country
if the Commission agrees that such a local market
is threatened.

5 The Efficiency of the Merger Process

A further elucidation is necessary to take into
account the argument of many economists that
mergers and take-overs are notoriously unsuccessful. This might be conducive to what has been
termed the anti-merger approach, under which all
mergers effected by companies above a certain size
are banned, unless substantial net social benefits
can be demonstrated, or failing firms are involved.[8]

---

[8] See Chiplin, B. and Wright, M. 1987: *The logic of mergers*, Hobart paper 107, published by the Institute of Economic Affairs, London, pp. 78 *et seq*. They make a distinction
between a pro-merger, a trade-off, a competitive structure
and an anti-merger approach.

Many investigations have established that about half the mergers undertaken are, in the end, "a disappointing marriage" (R. Meeks); they have to be rated an outright failure, or at best, not worthwhile. It is indeed the case that the many studies which economists have devoted to the outcome of mergers show a 40–40–20 (or 45–45–10) result: successes and failures are about evenly divided, and the rest turned out to be unprofitable events.

My question relates to the interpretation of these ratios. Given these outcomes of merger activity, can it be said that mergers and take-overs are wasteful, and a drain on the efficiency of the firms effecting them? A failure rate of some 40 percent is not a glorious record, and research also suggests that an increasing frequency of merger activity and a higher proportion of less related or unrelated mergers further diminishes the positive results. But the question remains: what is the standard of judgment? If we compare the success rate of merger activity with that of other risky business activities, the comparison is not so bad. Of innovated products brought onto the market, 70 to 80 percent are said to fail within five years; of newly starting small firms, some 50 percent in Great Britain and the Netherlands fail within six years; in the US, 60 percent.[9] Even firms established as subsidiaries by the largest companies have a failure rate which is

[9] Adolf, S. C. and Stokman, C. T. M. 1985: *Innovatie en MKB*. Amsterdam: Deelrapport 2, p. 64; Burns, P. and Dewhurst, J. 1986: Great Britain and N. Ireland. In *Small*

probably as high as some two-thirds to three-quarters that of mergers.[10] Thus, while it is true that mergers and take-overs have an extra risk dimension in comparison with internal growth, the rate of failure is nevertheless not particularly high in comparison with other economic activities where an element of newness is significant. Such a conclusion is at odds with both the market power and the efficiency theories of the merger process. From my own point of view, both these types of theory are one-sided and inadequate as explanations of the high, but not excessive, failure rates of combination movements. Both theories would have us think that the success rate of mergers is far higher than it really is. Moreover, from a competition policy point of view, the failure rate, whether high or low, is not particularly relevant in a free market economy, in which businesses must take responsibility for the outcomes of their actions.

6 The Market for Corporate Control

There is one domain in merger policy where the above maxim does not seem to apply, and which is

---

business in Europe. London: p. 64; Philips, B. D. and Kirchoff, B. A. 1989: Formation, growth and survival: Small firm dynamics in the US economy. In Small Business Economics, vol. 1, p. 69.

[10] Porter, M. E. 1987: From competitive advantage to corporate strategy. Harvard Business Review, May–June.

quickly gaining in importance, especially within the context of European integration. This is that area of widely diverging views and institutions, in the several countries, with respect to the value of free markets in corporate control. The question concerns whether a free take-over market (friendly or unfriendly) should exist or not, and in particular whether contested bids should be admitted. Broadly conceived, I think the views can be divided into three groups.

First, in the UK and the USA, the competitive bidding process for firms quoted on a stock exchange is considered a normal aspect of the business scene, and, even though firms have developed a whole arsenal of defensive measures against assailants, in the end these do not prevail, because of the law protecting the rights of shareholders, the great liquidity of the stock exchanges, and the rising influence of institutional investors such as pension funds and insurance companies.

The second group is constituted by West Germany, Sweden, the Netherlands, Switzerland, and Japan; in these countries there is no free market for corporate control, and contested bids are, for various reasons,[11] impossible to carry out.

[11] In the Netherlands, the corporate law puts final decision power into the hands of the board of directors. Shareholders, even if there is a clear majority, have no power to dismiss or reinstate executive directors. In addition, priority shares, non-voting certificates and preferential shares severely limit

The third group is formed by countries such as France and Belgium, where take-over bids are possible and do occur, but are infrequent, irregular, and of uncertain outcome: as the *Financial Times* wrote, "The gaps in the French rulebook ... mean that the outcome of any bid is highly uncertain."[12] The battle for Télémécanique in 1988 illustrates the point: the better bid by Schneider was held up for four-and-a-half months by government intervention, during which the stock exchange quotations were suspended; and recently

---

shareholder voting rights in most Dutch companies. Large West German companies have the big banks and some insurance companies as their main shareholders, whose influence is increased by large blocks of proxy votes entrusted to them by individual shareholders. See *Wirtschaft und Wettbewerb*, September 1989, pp. 697–704.

Swiss corporations issue registered and non-registered shares; the latter have no voting power. Corporation law permits managerial boards to refuse registered shareholder status, without stating a reason.

Swedish corporations cannot be acquired by foreigners without government permission; shares held by foreigners normally carry reduced voting rights.

The Japanese system is notoriously opaque. There is frequent intertwining of shareholdings between networks of corporations; additionally, the acquisition by foreigners of 10 percent or more of the shares in a company has to be registered with the government. A fundamental survey is given by Aoki, M. (ed.) 1984: *The economic analysis of the Japanese firm*. Amsterdam: pp. 9–31.

[12] *Financial Times*, 11 April, 1988.

the French Government prevented Spontex, a household sponge manufacturer, from falling into US hands: one could entertain the thought that sponges are considered a strategic material in France, the more so as the Competition Council advised favorably. Apart from government interference, and the frequently changing stock exchange rules, the three protective systems of "cascading," "auto-contrôle," and "verrouillage" severely limit successful take-over bids.[13]

Such important differences in corporate institutional arrangements have a predictable effect upon the market behavior of UK and US companies on the one hand, and of the Continental European, and Japanese, corporations on the other hand. The contrast is that between profit maximization and sales or growth maximization. The question is, can this polarity be made visible empirically? Table 2.2 illustrates the sales growth and profit rates of the leading 20 firms in the five major industrialized countries, with the Netherlands added for compa-

[13] "Cascading" is the way in which a parent company controls a successive chain of subsidiary companies by means of minority participation; "auto-contrôle" refers to inter-company structures in which a parent company's shares are held by its subsidiaries, while "verrouillage" is the locking-up of a large part of the shares of a company in a few, friendly hands. It is said that nearly two-thirds of the companies quoted on the Paris Bourse have half their capital in the hands of fewer than ten shareholders (*Financial Times*, 5 July, 1989).

Table 2.2 Sales and profits of the largest firms

	No of firms	1988 Sales profit (in billions of dollars)		Sales growth 1979–88 (%)	Profit rate (net profit/sales)			Rate of corporation tax	Corrected profit rate 1979–88
		Sales	profit		1979	1985	1988		
UK	20	253.6	20.3	45.4	6.1	3.6	8.0	35	9.01
W Germany	20	320.9	7.8	80.2	1.4	1.9	2.4	56	4.31
France	20	212.0	9.1	51.4	2.7	0.4	4.3	45	4.49
Netherlands	11	119.9	6.1	52.9	5.4	3.6(2.0)	5.1(4.7)	43	8.24(5.49)
Japan	20	383.0	9.3	190.6	1.9	2.9	2.4	43.3	4.23
US	20	770.6	45.6	48.0	5.0	4.9	5.9	46	9.75

Source: Fortune 500.

rative purposes. For each of the five countries, the 20 leading companies were traced in the *Fortune* 500 lists for the years 1979, 1985 and 1988. These were cyclically favorable years in each country, excluding misrepresentation, e.g., by means of under-utilized capacities, which might impair profitability. For the Netherlands, only 11 to 13 leading companies could be traced; these included Shell and Unilever, both of which were divided equally between the UK and the Netherlands. The profit rate figures in brackets indicate what occurs when both of these profitable companies, which are more American and British than Continental in their behavior, are eliminated from the Dutch group.

The average net profit rate for the three years was corrected for the differences in corporation tax,[14] and the last column gives the corrected profit rates. The table brings out the inverse relationship between sales growth during the period 1979 to 1988 (very high for the leading firms in West Germany and Japan, low for UK and US firms), and the profit rate (rather low in Continental Europe and Japan, high for UK and US corporations). The extraordinary sales growth of the leading West German and Japanese firms cannot be ascribed to growth in the GDP or industrial output of those countries, for West German growth was lower than in both the UK and the USA, and the higher

[14] The rates of which were derived the OECD publication, *Taxation in developed countries*, 1987, p. 87.

[64]

Japanese national economic growth can at best explain only half the rise of the 190 percent actual growth rate in sales of the 20 largest Japanese firms. The explanation of the inverse relationship would seem to be simply that West German and Japanese firms are sales maximizers, whereas the leading UK and US companies are profit maximizers. A similar investigation of the 40 leading companies in the major countries, and including the leading 10 to 20 companies in Sweden and Switzerland, gives practically the same results. The reason for this important difference in behavior is provided by the existence or otherwise of a market for corporate control. The threat of a (hostile) takeover bid puts pressure on the management of an American or British company to strive for profit maximization in a way that is not experienced by Continental European or Japanese companies.

This difference creates a problem for the future liberalization of international capital markets, and for European integration. It also raises the problem of reciprocity, and it may well be that growing US uneasiness, apparent, for instance, in the Exon–Florio Amendment to the 1988 Trade Act, and in the recent activation of the 1958 Airline Act, is inspired by such unevenness in treatment. I will not, however, take up these thorny political issues,[15] but concentrate on the relationship be-

[15] See the *Financial Times'* survey of the different systems in European capitalism, contained in "The Future of European capital markets," 5 July, 1989.

tween competition policy affecting mergers and the free market for corporate control.

7 Competition Policy and the Market for Corporate Control

It is said by some economists that merger policies and a free market for corporate control are in conflict: the more the corporate control market has its way, the less need there is for merger policies. Such an argument neglects the fact that take-over bids can establish a monopolistic or dominant position which is not restrained by the market for corporate control. Also, an already dominant firm may be acquired, without losing its market controlling position. In both cases, the market for corporate control mechanism simply transfers the current monopoly rents to the acquirers, or the capitalized monopoly profits to the owners who sell out, depending on the outcome of negotiations.

Some argue that a strong competition policy makes a market for corporate control, with its speculative and costly take-over battles, superfluous; but this view would seem to overrate the powers of the competition authorities to control the course of events, and, in any case, does not distinguish between the two separate kinds of problem which both systems are meant to solve.

[66]

My view is that merger policies and the market for corporate control are functionally more in addition to each other than substitutive in solving the merger problem. The first type of policy is designed to prevent monopolistic or non-contestable positions from arising in the first place, and, in case they have become a reality, to deal with them – for example, by means of *ex post facto* dissolution, or the divestment of parts of the dominant group, or the stipulation of behavioral conditions. The latter – i.e., the corporate control market – exists for correcting managerial failures and inefficiencies, and has no relevance to the competitive issues. Thus both types of policy are complementary and, together with management buy-outs or buy-ins, cover the various aspects of the merger problem: mergers may suppress as well as promote competition, and likewise reduce or enhance efficiency; thus, we do need two separate control mechanisms for handling the negative deviations of business strategy.

A further point reverses the question totally: if companies are free from the threat of take-over, they have a habit – as table 2.2 showed – of pursuing sales or growth maximization. This should reduce – it is said – the danger of monopolization, because the protected firms would tend to oversupply their product markets, and prices would, perhaps, decline to, or even below, marginal cost. Hence there would be less need for competition policy. Such an argument is most probably misconceived, however. Only if the world could be considered to be a unified market, with no or small transaction costs, an absence of barriers to penetration, and equal access to information, would the proposition seem to have validity. But in such a world, the distinction between sales or growth maximization and profit maximization would vanish altogether, because any growth or sales maximization strategy would run foul on a bid from a profit maximizing firm. We need to be reminded that in a free market economy, the achievement of profits is the only tenable long-run strategy; whatever else belongs to management's arsenal of strategies is connected with blockages to free trade. In the real world, such barriers do exist, which means that firms can pursue growth or sales maximization strategies without being penalized. Even worse, they can let the domestic consumer or foreign competing firms pay for those strategies, which cannot be reversed. The foreign dumping policies of Japanese concerns – like those of the pre-war German cartels – are a case in point: these strategies can only be pursued because those relatively unprofitable firms are immune from bids by profit maximizing foreign firms. It is no use to claim, as ultra free market economists do, that the subsidies involved in dumping benefit consumers in the non-protected country, because these subsidies distort the competitive process and may lead to artifically expanded sectors of industry, and the suppression of others. Pre-war steel dumping prevented the Dutch and Italian steel industries from growing naturally, and over-expanded their ship-building industries. Both tendencies were forcefully reversed when the European Coal and Steel Community was instituted, and the pendulum swung the other way. Likewise, Japanese dumping, for example of electronic goods, hampers the development of European and American manufacturing industry, and subsidizes the distribution sector with artificially cheap imports. Low or zero profitability in the dumped sectors then prompts the firms in those sectors to implement or call for protective measures, because they have become vulnerable to take-over. As usual, we get a cascading of the artificialities.

8 Concluding Remarks

What should European policy be in such circumstances? That is an intricate problem which cannot be solved in a few lines. However, an adequate solution most probably requires the integration of several policies directed towards the achievement of a free market process. Partial solutions only lead to further deterioration of performance. For example, the exclusive application of anti-dumping duties weakens the competitive discipline on European firms. The exclusive operation of a market for corporate control would lead to a cheap sell-out of our leading firms, and the loss of market shares. And anti-merger policies directed against foreigners, whether or not under the pretext of "the national interest" (for example US airlines, or French sponge manufacturers), only give cause for retaliation.

The EC, as one of the largest economic blocs in the world, should pursue a consistent program of free trade in goods, services and companies, both inside the Community and in relation to third countries. Inside the Community, conditions for orderly traffic, such as equality of treatment, transparency, and the need for bringing out a full bid once certain thresholds are passed, should be required, as well as the abolition of all artificial defense measures. In traffic with third countries, such as Japan, the US, Sweden, or Switzerland, the EC should insist on reciprocity, but not in a protectionist vein. As the largest trading bloc in the world, it should take the initiative in offering liberalization and free access to those countries which are ready to join the process. We should remember that reciprocity was a clause attached to trading agreements in the nineteenth century, used as an effective way to promote free trade.

3

Lessons from UK Merger Policy

K. D. GEORGE

3

Introduction

Mergers are a major factor in increases in concentration. This is confirmed by several studies. Although the most extreme estimates, which purport to show that mergers account for the whole of the increase in concentration, must be heavily discounted, the consensus that emerges from UK studies is clear enough: typically mergers have contributed to upwards of 50 percent of the increase in concentration over the relevant study periods and company samples.[1]

An increase in concentration does not, of course,

---

[1] See, for instance, Aaronovitch, S. and Sawyer, M. 1975: Mergers, growth and concentration. *Oxford Economics Papers*, March; Hannah, L. and Kay, J. A. 1977: *Concentration in Modern Industry: Theory Measurement and the UK Experience*. London: Macmillan; and Curry, B. and George, K. D. 1983: Industrial Concentration: A Survey. *Journal of Industrial Economics*, XXXI, March.

mean that monopoly power has necessarily increased correspondingly, or indeed at all. Any tendency towards increased market power may be offset by more vigorous enforcement of restrictive practices legislation, or by the widening of markets as a result of lower tariff and non-tariff barriers to trade. In addition, many mergers between small and medium-sized enterprises may strengthen competition by creating stronger rivals to dominant firms.

Increased levels of concentration may also lead to greater efficiency, and may do so in three distinct ways: by allowing greater exploitation of economies of scale and of scope; by internalizing activities that involve high transaction costs; and by concentrating activity in the hands of the most able managers.

But there is also plenty of room for concern about any long-term trend towards more concentrated markets. In particular, there are competitive risks to mergers, especially those resulting in greater horizontal and vertical integration. A reduction alone in the number of competitors may itself push up prices, by facilitating collusion, both explicit and tacit, and further welfare losses may be associated with a reduction in consumer choice.

Nor are the efficiency benefits mentioned earlier always achieved. In all cases of merger, they are potential rather than definite. Were this not so, many UK industries, such as the motor vehicle and machine tool industries, would not have suffered such catastrophic failure. The realization of economies of scale, associated, for instance, with longer production runs, requires conscious management effort to rationalize and restructure production. Benefits stemming from the internalization of transactions depend on management skills in communication, coordination and motivation, plus sufficient flexibility within the organization concerned to respond to changing conditions of demand and supply. Predators may have motives other than the maximization of shareholder interests. Merger activity may absorb a large proportion of managerial time, and place undue emphasis on short-term survival strategy at the expense of long-term strategic planning.[2]

These concerns have been largely brushed aside by the recent theorizing of the so-called "new industrial economics." Amongst the main strands of the new wisdom are the following:

1 Causality runs not from structure to performance, but in the reverse direction; i.e., high concentration and high market share, whether due to internal growth or merger, is a sign of efficiency, not of vice, reflecting the success of low-cost firms in expanding market share at the expense of less efficient competitors.

[2] For a general discussion and review of these matters, see Jacquemin, Buigues, and Ilzkovitz, 1989.

2 High profits are a short-run phenomenon, and are a necessary part of the competitive process. However, this process works speedily to eliminate monopoly profits, by attracting new entry and the search for close substitutes.

3 Barriers to entry have been exaggerated, the only effective barriers being those imposed by the state.

4 With the exception of markets where state-imposed entry barriers exist, potential competition is more important than actual competition within the market as the important constraint on monopoly behavior.[3]

These views are evident in some of the recent reports of the UK Monopolies and Mergers Commission.[4] If they were to be adopted by all those concerned with anti-trust matters, there would be little need for any form of competition

[3] On these points see, for instance, Peltzman, S. 1977: The Gains and Losses from Industrial Concentration. *Journal of Law and Economics*, 20; Baumol, W. J., Panzar J. C., and Willig, R. D. 1982: *Contestable Markets and the Theory of Industrial Structure*. New York: Harcourt Brace Jovanovich; Littlechild, S. C. 1986: *The Fallacy of the Mixed Economy*. Hobart Paper 80, London: Institute of Economic Affairs, London.

[4] See, for instance, the Monopolies and Mergers Commission reports on *Postal Franking Machines* (1986) and *Tampons* (1986) (London: HMSO).

[76]

policy. However, as an attempt to model real world markets, the new wisdom is seriously flawed. It ignores or minimizes market imperfections which can be exploited by large firms, and in particular puts too much emphasis on potential competition, and too little on actual competition. Evaluation of the intensity of potential competition is highly subjective. There are severe difficulties in evaluating the nature and height of entry barriers, of identifying potential entrants, and the extent and speed of entry, should it occur.[5] This is not to deny the importance of the competitive process and the part played in it by profits and new entry. The key issue is the speed with which (and indeed the direction in which) the competitive process works. The evidence is that, although there is a tendency for monopoly power to decay, this is often a slow process, and until this happens completely, the economy suffers the costs of higher prices and lower efficiency.[6]

---

[5] For an attack on the "new IO theories" and a defense of "mainstream" industrial organization, see Shepherd, W. G. 1989: *The Process of Effective Competition*. Working Paper, 1. University of Massachusetts: Department of Economics.

[6] On the persistence of monopoly, see Shaw, R. and Simpson P. 1986: The persistence of monopoly: an investigation of the effectiveness of the UK Monopolies Commission. *Journal of Industrial Economics*, 34; Geroski, P. A. 1987: Do dominant firms decline? In Hay, D. A. and Vickers, J. S. (eds) *The Economics of Market Dominance*. Oxford: Basil Blackwell.

1 The Framework of Law and Policy

Merger policy in the UK dates from the passing of the Monopolies and Mergers Act, 1965; the current merger control provisions are contained in the Fair Trading Act, 1973. There have been government reviews of policy in 1978 and 1988, but the basis for policy has remained largely unaltered.

The present machinery of control is one in which three authorities perform distinct roles. These authorities are the Director General of the Office of Fair Trading, the Secretary of State for Trade and Industry, and the Monopolies and Mergers Commission (MMC).

The Director General has a duty to keep himself informed of all mergers – actual or prospective – and to advise the Secretary of State on whether a "qualifying merger" should be referred to the MMC. A qualifying merger is one where the merged companies constitute a legal monopoly because they will control at least 25 percent of the UK market, or where the value of assets taken over exceeds a specified threshold (currently 30 million pounds).

The Office of Fair Trading (OFT) learns about mergers from the press, or from informal notification of merger proposals by the parties. The OFT has four to six weeks in which to complete initial inquiries and to tender advice to the Secretary of State. In complex cases, the Director General will

[78]

receive advice from the Mergers Panel, an inter-departmental committee with representation from all interested government departments.

If a merger is referred by the Secretary of State, the MMC is required to report on whether it operates, or may be expected to operate, against the public interest. The guidance given for interpreting the public interest is extremely wide, and is the same as that applied in monopoly investigations, as laid down in Section 84(1) of the Fair Trading Act. It states that: "the Commission shall take into account all matters which appear to them in the particular circumstances to be relevant . . . ." The MMC takes evidence from the firms involved in the merger, their customers, competitors, trade unions, and other interested parties. The onus of proof is on the MMC to demonstrate that a merger might be expected to operate against the public interest, and in so doing it must be able to demonstrate specific adverse effects.

The MMC has no power itself to stop a merger. If it concludes that a merger might be expected not to operate against the public interest, there is no power at all to stop the merger. If it concludes that a merger is against the public interest, the power to stop it rests with the Secretary of State. The MMC can only recommend what action should be taken – i.e., whether to stop a merger, or to allow it subject to certain undertakings. In order for the Secretary of State to exercise his powers there must be an adverse public interest finding, but he decides at his discretion whether to accept the conclusion and recommendations of the MMC. In deciding what action to take, the Secretary of State will again be advised by the Director General of the OFT.

The review of merger policy that took place in 1988 recommended no radical changes.[7] The review noted the criticism that merger control procedures have been time-consuming and inflexible, welcomed the progress made in cutting the length of MMC investigations, and declared that some of the proposed improvements in working methods and internal procedures would require minor legislative changes. In addition, two more substantial legislative changes were announced. The first was "a formal, though non-mandatory, pre-notification procedure" designed to secure the rapid clearance of mergers where there are no grounds for a referral. Those who decide to pre-notify their proposed merger to the OFT will be required to complete a standard questionnaire, setting out basic information about the transaction and about the business involved. In simple cases, and provided the proposed merger has been publicly announced so that third parties have an opportunity to register objections, the merger will be given automatic clearance if nothing is heard from the OFT within a short period – possibly only four weeks. In more com-

[7] Department of Trade and Industry 1988: *Mergers Policy.* London: HMSO.

plex cases it will take longer for the OFT to assess the position, and in these cases firms will be informed that the right to automatic clearance does not apply. Mergers which are not pre-notified will remain liable to referral to the MMC for a period of up to five years. The idea of a mandatory pre-notification procedure for mergers above a certain size was rejected because of the additional burden that would be involved, both for the authorities and for business; because firms in any case often choose to inform the OFT of merger proposals, and because "it has been comparatively rare for completed mergers to raise issues which justify reference ...," although as the review admitted in the same sentence, "there have been a number of references of completed mergers in the recent past[!]" (par. 3.7). Voluntary pre-notification is, of course, not new to UK merger policy. However, the procedures proposed in the 1988 review give greater incentives for firms to pre-notify, and should improve the information available to the OFT.

The second major legislative proposal announced in the 1988 review was for the introduction of a mechanism whereby parties to a merger can give legally binding undertakings to meet competition objections, as an alternative to an MMC referral. Undertakings might involve divestment of some of the assets of the merging companies, or relate to the post-merger behavior of the new group. If the Director General is satisfied that the undertakings remove a possible adverse effect on competition, he can advise the Secretary of State against making a referral. If an undertaking to divest assets is not honored, the Secretary of State will have powers, without an MMC investigation, to require divestment. This addition to merger policy gives statutory backing to an apparently growing willingness of predators to divest themselves of assets in order to avoid an MMC reference. Thus, in their (unsuccessful) bid for the Imperial Group, United Biscuits announced their willingness to sell the Golden Wonder snack food division of Imperial, in order to reduce the merged company's share of the snack foods market to below 25 percent. In announcing its successful take-over bid for Distillers, Guinness agreed to sell several brands of whisky, in order to avoid creating a dominant position in the UK market. Indeed, the then chief executive of Guinness is reported to have said that the divestment was in the public interest, because it would stimulate competition in the UK market! As a final example, Dixons, in its unsuccessful bid for Woolworths, announced that it would dispose of the Comet electrical chain in order to avoid a possible reference to the MMC.

2 Issues

PERMISSIVENESS OF UK POLICY

The underlying attitude of UK merger policy is that most mergers are beneficial, but that a small number may be against the public interest, and thus need to be investigated. In 1969 the minister then responsible for merger policy stated that "in general mergers are desirable if they lead to better management or genuine economies of scale without eliminating workable competition. In my view more often than not in Britain mergers will fulfil this condition."[8] This continues to be the government's view. Thus in the 1988 White Paper, *DTI – the Department for Enterprise*, it is stated that the policy towards mergers "enables the great majority of proposed mergers and acquisitions which do not pose a threat to competition to be decided by the market, without intervention from official agencies." Thus, in mergers as in monopolies legislation, the presumption is against public intervention.

The permissive attitude towards mergers is reflected in the fact that the onus of proof is on the Commission to show that a merger would be against public interest, and also in the number of mergers which have been referred to the Commission. The figures show that over the period 1977–87, 57 referrals (including ten newspaper referrals) were made out of a total number of approximately 2,493 mergers covered by the legislation, or 2.3 percent of all referrable cases, and less than 1 percent of all industrial and commercial mergers. There are a number of possible explanations for the

[8] See Board of Trade 1969: *Mergers: A guide to Board of Trade Practice*. London: HMSO, annex 5.

permissive attitude that has been adopted towards mergers.

First, there has been an uncritical association of efficiency with size, irrespective of *how* large size is attained. Merger proposals are invariably supported by claims of efficiency gains due to economies of large-scale production, or economies in distribution and marketing. However, these advantages are more easily claimed than realized, and research into the matter tends to show disappointing results.[9]

Secondly, there is the view that the take-over mechanism is an efficient selection mechanism, weeding out inefficiency, and concentrating resources in the most efficiently managed firms. At best, however, UK research in this area gives only highly qualified support to this view. Studies show a tendency for acquired firms to be smaller and less dynamic than other groups, and to have lower profitability, especially in the years immediately preceding a take-over, suggesting perhaps opportunistic behavior on the part of the acquirers. Acquiring companies tend on average to be larger and faster-growing than other firms, but profitability comparisons lead to less clear-cut conclusions. When acquired and acquiring companies are compared, size is the clearest discriminator, with profitability comparisons again showing mixed results.

[9] See, for instance, Cowling, K. et al. 1980: *Mergers and Economic Performance*. Cambridge University Press.

Whatever general tendencies are found are usually rather weak, with substantial overlap occurring in the performance of groups of firms.[10]

Thirdly, there is the argument that because the future is uncertain, and industrial structure is constantly adapting itself to changing circumstances, the success rate of predicting the effects of mergers is likely to be low. Since most mergers are likely to be pro-competitive or neutral in their effects, it is best to replace merger control with control of the undesirable conduct of monopolies when such conduct appears.[11] However, there are a number of difficulties in adopting this view. The argument that mergers are pro-competitive is not convincing when internal growth is a feasible alternative, or when a merger destroys an effective competitor, or weakens potential competition, or raises entry barriers.

The empirical work on the effects of mergers is also not reassuring. Most investigators in the UK have concluded that post-merger profitability performance has been worse than pre-merger performance in a small majority of cases. Certainly there is usually a finding that a large minority of mergers are "successful" on the basis of these tests,

[10] These are some of the findings in Singh, A. 1975: Takeovers, economic natural selection and the theory of the firm. *Economic Journal*, September; Meeks, G., 1977; and Kumar, K. S. 1984: *Growth, Acquisition and Investment*. Cambridge University Press.
[11] See, for instance, Littlechild, S. C., 1986.

and also that the quantitative decline in post-merger profitability is typically small. Nevertheless, the results do not support an optimistic view of the effects of mergers.[12] Studies based on share price movements appear to give more reassuring results. Much of the evidence relating to share prices in the short period immediately before and after a merger shows substantial gains to the shareholders of acquired firms, and gains also, albeit on a much more modest scale, to the shareholders of acquiring firms. However, if these share price movements are supposed to reflect the potential for longer-term gains in efficiency and profitability, it is odd that there is so little direct evidence of such gains in studies based on company accounts, which were referred to earlier. In this context it is interesting to note that, when share price movements are examined over a longer period, the picture becomes less clear-cut. Much of the evidence then suggests that the short-term gains are not sustained.[13]

The experience of UK monopoly policy is also not reassuring when it comes to correcting abuses of market power. The UK authorities have only once, for instance, resorted to the structural rem-

[12] See, for instance, Meeks, G., 1977; Kumar, K. S., 1984; and Hughes, A. 1989: The Impact of Merger: A Survey of Empirical Evidence for the UK. In Fairburn, J. A. and Kay, J. A. (eds) *Mergers and Merger Policy*. Oxford University Press.

[13] See Hughes, A., 1989.

[86]

edy of divestment of assets as a means of correcting monopoly abuse. Wherever possible, and especially where structural remedies are regarded as impractical, it is better to prevent the emergence of market power, than to attempt to modify business behavior and performance once such power has emerged, and this suggests the need for a stronger merger policy.[14]

A permissive attitude towards mergers seems to have been adopted by the European Commission. The preamble to the draft EC regulation, for instance, seems to encourage mergers: "the dismantling of internal frontiers can be expected to result in major corporate reorganisations in the Community, particularly in the form of concentrations ... and such a development must be welcomed as being in line with the requirements of dynamic competition and liable to strengthen the competitiveness of European industry ...."[15] There is, however, a danger that some of the benefits of a wider and freer market in Europe will be lost, as firms scramble to assert their market power through mergers, a danger that is increased by the sort of encouraging statement just referred to.

[14] For a discussion of these issues see George, K. D. 1989: Do we need a Merger Policy? In Fairburn, J. A. and Kay, J. A. (eds) *Mergers and Merger Policy*. Oxford University Press.

[15] Commission of the European Communities 1988: *Amended proposal for a Council regulation on the control of concentrations between undertakings*. Brussels.

[87]

Mergers, in certain circumstances, may be necessary for successful rationalization, restructuring and modernization, but it can be expected that businessmen will greatly exaggerate the need for them.

PROCEDURES FOR MAKING REFERRALS

The decision whether or not to refer a merger is made by the Secretary of State on advice from the Director General of Fair Trading. This advice is usually taken, but not invariably so. From 1979 to 1988 there were nine occasions where the Director General's advice on referrals was not accepted by the Secretary of State. For instance, in 1979 the Secretary of State decided not to accept the Director General's advice that the merger between Thorn Electrical Industries and EMI be referred, and in 1982 decided to refer A. J. Lewis's bid for Illingworth Morris, against his advice. Examples of insignificant mergers that have been referred are the bids for Sotheby's (1983) and the proposed merger of two manufacturers of snuff(!) (1985) – which subsequently lapsed before the MMC inquiry started. These cases raise the question of the politicization of the referral process, and whether the power to refer would not be better vested in the OFT than in the hands of the Secretary of State.

Apart from defining mergers eligible for referral

in terms of the market share and asset tests, UK legislation lays down no statutory criteria for making referrals. The Secretary of State may refer any case where he thinks there is an important public interest issue at stake – this may relate to regional issues, the balance of payments, foreign ownership, or the proposed method of financing a merger, as well as to the effect on competition. In 1984, however, the Secretary of State announced that referrals were to be made "primarily on competition grounds," and that in evaluating the competitive situation in individual cases, regard would be paid to "the extent of competition in the home market from non-United Kingdom sources and to the competitive position of United Kingdom companies in overseas markets."[16] The problem of the breadth of the public interest criterion is dealt with later. Here our concern is with the absence of any clear set of guidelines for dealing with competition referrals.

There is much to be said in favor of deciding referrals within a publicly-known set of guidelines. These would inevitably be based mainly on market shares and concentration levels relating to sales in the UK market – thus allowing for imports. A minimum market size might also usefully be specified, in order to eliminate trivial referrals. Data on these dimensions of market structure would be

---

[16] Extract from a written answer by the Secretary of State, Mr N. Tebbit, to a Parliamentary Question, July 1984.

used as part of an initial screening procedure designed to pinpoint those cases where there is a possibility of a serious restriction or distortion of competition, and which would therefore automatically be challenged. These dimensions of structure would no doubt need to be supplemented by other considerations. One such consideration would be the trend in the market shares of the merging firms; another would be the rate of growth of the market. Where demand is expanding rapidly, internal growth will be an inducement to investment in capacity extensions and in R & D. In a declining industry, on the other hand, particularly one with a highly competitive market structure, there may be serious obstacles to the internal growth of firms, and the case for mergers may be strong. Such an industry may be characterized by chronic excess capacity because of the slow adjustment of capacity to demand, an aged capital stock, and generally poor-quality managment. In these circumstances, a merger may improve efficiency by encouraging the scrapping of old machines and investment in new ones, by reducing the uncertainty associated with excess capacity and by increasing the proportion of the industry's assets under the control of efficient managers.

One argument in favor of using a set of guidelines is that it would create greater certainty for the business community in relation to the application of policy. It would also assist in achieving greater consistency in applying that policy. It is at the pre-referral stage of merger policy that the greatest scope exists for a consistent approach, because by their very nature the cases that are referred should be the ones where the pros and the cons are more finely balanced and where, therefore, it is more difficult to reach a clear verdict.

In this respect the EC draft regulation is an improvement, in that it focuses attention on those mergers with a Community dimension which "create or strengthen a dominant position" – a more precise concept than making referrals on "competition grounds." But the criteria suggested for determining dominance are too vague, and could be given more precision, especially in relation to such matters as market shares and levels of concentration.

DEFINING THE MARKET

The use of market guidelines presupposes a meaningful definition of markets. This is an old and familiar problem in economics which, although dealt with easily enough in theory, has never been satisfactorily dealt with in practice, because of measurement problems. The guidelines currently in use in the United States define the relevant market as a "group of products ... for which a hypothetical monopolist could profitably impose a small but significant and nontransitory increase in price," the hypothetical price increase normally to be applied being 5 percent, and lasting one year. The market is properly defined when such a price increase would not be thwarted by consumer substitution, or entry of other producers into the market. The guidelines point out that in defining markets in this way, it will usually be necessary to infer likely effects from various bits of circumstantial evidence. These include buyers' and sellers' perceptions of the market, actual price movements, and similarities or differences in usage, design and physical characteristics.[17] The US approach leans heavily on the concept of potential substitution in demand and supply, and is open to the objection referred to earlier: namely that primary emphasis should be given to actual competition, rather than to the more subjective estimates of potential competition.

Even then, market definition is not an exact science, and inevitably requires the use of qualitative as well as quantitative evidence. Both the OFT and MMC have come in for criticism for the way in which they have tackled the problem. For instance, in recent merger cases relating to mail order, bricks, and textile maintenance, one authority criticized the Commission for offering "no quantitative evidence on the substitutability between goods obtained by mail order or other forms of retailing; linen hire or other forms of

[17] See US Department of Justice 1984: *Merger Guildelines*, June 14.

obtaining clean linen; flatten bricks and other bricks."[18] It is indeed true that the MMC did not in any of these cases offer evidence of cross-elasticities of demand, but then reliable estimates of this type are hardly ever available. However, the Commission did, in all three cases, consider the sort of circumstantial evidence which is mentioned in the US guidelines.

With the approach of 1992, a complaint that is being increasingly heard is that the UK should no longer be regarded as distinct from the Community for competition purposes. However, while the relevant market may be the Community, or indeed the whole world, this is not invariably the case. Some goods and services are not traded; for those that are, there are wide variations in import penetration. Furthermore, foreign competition may be blunted by non-tariff barriers such as customer preferences, government procurement policies, different health and safety standards, and so on. At the macro level, exchange rate fluctuations cause additional uncertainty.

The problem of defining markets gives further emphasis to the point that merger guidelines are just that – an initial screening device to give greater consistency to policy, and to aid in the identification of cases where serious competition issues are likely to arise.

[18] Barna, T. 1984: Contradictions in Verdicts on Mergers. *Financial Times*, 5 March, 1984.

THE PUBLIC INTEREST

The public interest is defined very widely for the purposes of monopolies and mergers investigations. The MMC is instructed to take into account "all matters which appear to them in particular circumstances to be relevant ...," and among other things shall have regard to the desirability:

1 of maintaining and promoting effective competition;
2 of promoting the interests of consumers, purchasers and other users;
3 of promoting, through competition, the reduction of costs, the development and use of new techniques and new products, and facilitating new entry;
4 of maintaining and promoting the balanced distribution of industry and employment;
5 of maintaining and promoting competitive activity in markets outside the United Kingdom.

The guidelines have been criticized for being too wide, and for forcing the Commission into considering matters about which it is not well qualified.

The regional dimension of the public interest has featured in a number of referrals, particularly Lonrho/House of Frazer, the take-over bids for the Royal Bank of Scotland, and Charter Consolidated/Anderson Strathclyde. In the first of these the claim by the House of Frazer that the merger would have an adverse effect on the Scottish economy was dismissed by the Commission as not having sufficient weight. In the other two cases, the majority view on the Commission was that a merger would result in significant damage to the economy of Scotland. In both cases, emphasis was placed on the loss of employment that would ensue as a result of the change in status of the acquired company, from being independent to being a subsidiary of a large group. Regional problems are of course important, and there is some evidence that development is adversely affected if a region has a high proportion of its business in the form of branch factories or subsidiaries of companies whose headquarters are located elsewhere. However, regional problems can, and should, be dealt with more effectively with the aid of more appropriate policy weapons such as grants, loans and other regional incentives.

The same point can be made about the balance of payments effects of mergers. Once more, the claims and counter-claims made in evidence to the Commission are more than usually speculative, and difficult to assess. In the report on Car Parts, for instance, the UK car manufacturers and importers argued that the termination of the exclusive buying of replacement parts imposed by them

[95]

upon franchised dealers would have an adverse effect on imports and the balance of payments. However, representatives of the car components industry contested the view that they would be unable to compete with foreign suppliers. Once again, the important consideration is that more powerful and reliable weapons than competition policy are available for dealing with the balance of payments. Interestingly, in the Car Parts report the Commission concluded that, "even if it were established that the components industry and other industries dependent on it needed protection against foreign competition, the desirability of providing it and the method of doing so should be matters of considered government policy and should not be left to the operation of an anti-competitive practice adopted to further sectional commercial interest."

There is a widespread view that the open-ended approach to defining the objectives of competition policy is a fundamental weakness in enforcement decision-making. A possible solution would be to restrict the relevant matters in monopoly and merger references to those that are contained in paragraphs (a), (b) and (c) of Section 84(1) of the 1973 Act, and which are summarized in points 1–3 above.

If the MMC is to be continued to be asked to investigate mergers in which the major issues relate to regional, balance of payments, or other non-competition problems, it would be better for these

[96]

to be treated as special cases outside the mainstream of merger referrals. The Enserch/Davy referral, for instance, would not have occurred on the basis of a concentration/market share guideline approach, because there was no question of any detriment arising out of reduced competition. The referral might have been made, however, on the basis of extraordinary circumstances relating to the national interest, and to export markets.

It has also been suggested that the MMC should not be concerned with the efficiency consequences of a merger. However, unless the cost–benefit approach to mergers is to be abandoned altogether, it is essential that the likely efficiency consequences of mergers be taken into account, so that any anticipated gains can be weighed against any detriment to competition.

The EC draft regulation is firmly based on competitive issues, with provision for an efficiency defense as laid out in Article 2(3). It may seem surprising, therefore, that this has met with strong opposition from the UK authorities. The reason for this is twofold. First, the efficiency defense is widely drawn, and there is a fear that mergers may be approved for reasons of broad industrial and social strategy which may be damaging to competition. Secondly, although the efficiency defense is part of UK policy, the decision to allow a merger to proceed on the grounds that efficiency gains outweigh any anti-competitive detriment is made not by the MMC, but by the Secretary of

State, who is accountable to Parliament. The European Commission is not so accountable.

THE BURDEN OF PROOF AND RELATED MATTERS

In order to arrive at an adverse public interest finding, the MMC must specify particular effects, adverse to the public interest, which in the opinion of the MMC the proposed merger may be expected to have. The question is not merely whether there is a *possibility* that a merger will operate against the public interest; there must be an *expectation* that some particular effect adverse to the public interest will occur. On several occasions there has been some difficulty in arguing this with conviction, and mergers have been stopped on what have seemed to some observers to be trivial or even irrelevant grounds. In Lonrho/House of Frazer and Charter Consolidated/Anderson Strathclyde, for instance, emphasis was placed on the adverse effects the merger was expected to have on managerial efficiency. However, in these two cases, and others such as Enserch/Davy, Hepworth/Steetley and GKN/AE, a factor that influenced members of the MMC was either that the threatened company was efficient, or was showing clear signs of improved performance. However, since a merger cannot be blocked simply on the grounds that the company to be acquired is efficient, the MMC has to argue that the efficiency of the acquired company, the acquiring company or both, may be expected to be impaired as a result of the acquisition. It is then drawn inevitably into the thorny problem of evaluating relative management teams.

It would be far more satisfactory if the MMC were able to recommend that a merger be stopped because it would result in the elimination of a company which, on the evidence available, could be expected to operate successfully as an independent business. This would be in the spirit of existing legislation. The wording of Section 84(1)(c) of the 1973 Act is that the MMC should have regard to the desirability "of promoting, *through competition*, the reduction of costs and the development and use of new techniques ..." (author's italics). In other words, there would seem to be a presumption against the acceptance of arguments that these desirable goals are to be achieved by structural changes that are likely to lead to an enhancement of market power, at least if a viable and more competitive alternative is available. The preservation of effective competitors must be good for the maintenance of effective competition.

Many of these cases involve small and medium-sized enterprises (SMEs). An important strand running through the European Commission's thinking in recent years has been the conviction that special attention has to be given to SMEs as one way of preserving competitive market structures.[19] The Commission can, for instance, use Article 86 to prevent SMEs from being disadvantaged by the anti-competitive behavior of dominant firms. Consideration should be given to extending these powers, so as to limit the extent to which SMEs are swallowed up by giant predators. The point has been made that there are more appropriate and less costly methods of preserving the independence of companies – in particular, by persuading the financial institutions to take a more active interest in the companies in which they have invested, or by establishing supervisory boards along German lines.[20] Such mechanisms would reduce the role of the take-over bid in remedying managerial weaknesses, and would help preserve a larger number of well-managed companies. However, there is little sign of such institutional reforms taking place in the UK, and until there is, merger policy should have a role to play.

The problem of maintaining efficient competitors would be resolved, to some extent at least, by reversing the burden of proof. Ever since the inception of merger policy in the UK, it has been for the MMC to demonstrate adverse effects if a merger is to be blocked; firms do not have to

[19] See, for instance, Commission of the European Communities 1986: *Fifteenth Report on Competition Policy*. Brussels.
[20] See the introduction to Fairburn, J. A. and Kay, J. A. (eds) 1989: *Mergers and Merger Policy*. Oxford University Press.

[100]

demonstrate benefit. The MMC may find no material advantages to a merger, but no adverse effects either, in which case it must allow the merger to proceed.[21] There are good reasons for reversing the position. First, our starting point must be the desirability of maintaining effective competition; economic theory tells us that there are competitive risks associated with mergers. In addition, the weight of empirical evidence does not support a presumption in favor of mergers. When dealing with the relatively small number of cases that pose the greatest threat to competition, it would seem reasonable to place the burden of proof on the firms. There is a further point. The parties to a merger have more detailed knowledge of the circumstances than any outside body. They will also have (or should have) given careful thought to the key issues before launching a bid. They should be expected, therefore, to use this superior knowledge to demonstrate benefit. As things stand, however, firms do not have a sufficiently strong incentive to place a carefully presented case before the MMC.

---

[21] See, for instance, Monopolies and Mergers Commission 1985: *Scottish & Newcastle Breweries PLC and Matthew Brown PLC: A report on the proposed merger*. Cmnd 9645. London: HMSO. In par. 7.31 the MMC said: "We discern no material advantages to the public interest arising from the proposed merger; but the question before us is whether the merger may be expected to operate against the public interest and in our view there are not sufficient grounds for such an expectation."

Reversing the burden of proof would force companies to think more carefully about a proposed merger before proceeding.

One particular example of evidence which is rather badly presented to the Commission in many cases is the estimated efficiency gains expected from a merger. In this respect it is useful to distinguish between size, and the process of attaining large size. It may well be that the most important elements of increased efficiency are associated with the process of growth, rather than with size as such, and that the gains obtained simply by merging firms into larger units may be small.[22] This, however, is an empirical question, and firms should be required to estimate the extent to which costs will be reduced as a result of a merger, and to explain how the reductions will be achieved, and over what time-period.

The case for reversing the burden of proof was considered in 1978 by the Green Paper *A Review of Monopolies and Mergers Policy*, and rejected in favor of a neutral position, but no action was taken on this recommendation. It was argued that reversing the burden of proof would result in the MMC being swamped with referrals. The possibility of reversing the presumption for certain types of merger that give rise to particular concern, for

---

[22] For an elaboration of an argument along these lines, see Cyert, R. M. and George, K. D. 1969: Competition Growth and Efficiency. *Economic Journal*, March.

instance, those that create a large market share, or involve very large companies, was also rejected. It was argued that reversing the burden of proof for this sub-category:

would be a strong deterrent against bringing forward merger proposals above the threshold even though they might be desirable in the national interest. The much severer treatment of merger proposals above the threshold (choice of which would inevitably be arbitrary) would tend to distort companies' approach to mergers as those below the threshold came to be regarded as in some way better than those above it, and it cannot be assumed that the outcome would be the most favourable to the public interest.[23]

The 1988 review of merger policy also decided to leave the onus of proof unchanged. The defense of existing policy outlined in the review (paras 2.8–2.13) is that, given the presumption that the vast majority of mergers raise no competition or other objections, and are best left for the market to decide, "it would be inconsistent to reverse the burden of proof and to require those proposing a merger to demonstrate that this proposal would be positively in the public interest. This would make take-overs much harder to carry out, and would have a damaging effect on efficiency by weakening

[23] See *A Review of Monopolies and Mergers Policy: A Consultative Document.* Cmnd 7198. London: HMSO; 1978.

the discipline of the market over incumbent company managements."

These arguments are not convincing. Even with the onus of proof reversed, the vast majority of mergers would, as at present, be cleared quickly in the initial screening phase. Only those which, in the opinion of the OFT, presented a threat to competition, would be referred to the MMC. The severer treatment of merger proposals above some sensibly defined threshold is exactly what should be aimed at. (The "severer treatment" would need to come both in the preliminary vetting procedures of the OFT, and in the reversal of the burden of proof for those cases that were referred.) If we are not prepared to accept that, a priori, the greatest danger to competitive behavior comes from the most highly concentrated industries, there is not much of a basis left for policy. As to deterring large mergers, that again is a desirable outcome. There would be a strong disincentive for companies to come forward with merger proposals which rested on flimsy arguments. However, it would not deter merger proposals being made where the parties concerned felt that they had a convincing case. This is as it should be.

The case for reversing the burden of proof applies with even greater force at the Community level. After all, only those mergers with a Community dimension, and which pose the most serious threat to competition, will be challenged, and if the policy of maintaining effective competition is to be taken seriously, it is surely right in these few cases that the burden of proof should rest with the parties to a merger.

MMC INVESTIGATIONS

The MMC has come in for a lot of criticism over the time taken on merger investigations. The point has also been made that the mere referral of a proposed merger may jeopardize the transaction. To some extent, of course, these problems are inherent in any merger policy.

Up to 1986 the time taken to complete a merger referral was typically six months or more. Since then, as a result of tighter procedures, it has been reduced to three or four months. Although it is clearly desirable that referrals be completed as expeditiously as possible, there must also be regard to the duties of the MMC. The Commission has to prepare a report for the Secretary of State, who has to decide whether or not to accept its recommendations. The report must contain all that the MMC wishes to say, and must therefore contain enough material to explain and support its conclusions. The Commission has a duty to act fairly, and to ensure that every party that appears before it is given a fair opportunity to state its case and to comment on allegations made against it. As a past Chairman of the MMC has argued:

[105]

it is desirable ... that merger inquiries should not be unnecessarily prolonged. However, the principal public interest must be that merger control be effective and acceptable. It cannot be effective unless it is based upon thorough investigation of the circumstances and full consideration of the advantages and disadvantages alleged in each case. It is unlikely to be acceptable unless it provides fair treatment of the parties and fair consideration of the arguments they wish to present. There would be no public advantage in any time limits which might make it impossible for the Commission to act effectively and fairly in carrying out its inquiries.[24]

A period of several weeks or months is bound to be irksome to acquiring firms or to the parties to an agreed merger. But if merger control is to be conducted properly, it is inevitable. In any case it is worth repeating that the cases under consideration are those most likely to be damaging to competition, and that if there are substantial benefits to be attained from a merger, these are not likely to evaporate over the period of an inquiry.

Over the years, the MMC has succeeded very well in being both efficient in the conduct of its enquiries, and fair to all interested parties. To combine these attributes of efficiency and fairness will

[24] Le Quesne, Sir G. 1988: The Monopolies Commission at Work. In George, K. D. (ed.) *Macmillan's Mergers and Acquisition Yearbook*. London: Macmillan.

be a major challenge facing the European Commission in developing a Community merger policy.

The MMC has also been criticized (not always fairly) for its handling of competition issues. Sometimes the criticism is that it has got the competition issue wrong; sometimes that insufficient attention has been given to competition, or that other considerations have been given undue weight. Both facets appear, for instance, in the British Airways/British Caledonian referral. In this case the Commission took account of the greater opportunity an enlarged BA would have for anti-competitive behavior. However, it was more impressed by the arguments presented by BA – that the enlarged company would be operating in a highly competitive market, and that the merger would strengthen BA's competitive position *vis-à-vis* foreign airlines; that the integration of the operations of the two companies would lead to substantial operating economies, and that without the merger, BCal was in danger of liquidation or break-up, with consequent job losses. In its evidence to the Commission, the Civil Aviation Authority (CAA) was of the view that the merger would have little impact on BA's competitive position, and also that for an airline of BA's size, further size-related cost savings seemed unlikely. The point has also been made that the financial crisis facing BCal could have been dealt with by merger with another less-dominant international airline, but that the MMC took no account of that possibility.[25] Finally, insofar as job losses influenced the MMC, it could be argued that employment, like regional issues and the balance of payments, should not form part of the deliberations of a competition authority, there being other more effective weapons for dealing with the problem.

These observations on the BA/BCal investigation form a convenient background for one or two general comments about the MMC's handling of competition issues. In the first place, although successive Secretaries of State since 1984 have confirmed that referrals are made primarily on competition grounds, once a referral is made, there is no guarantee that the Commission will give competition issues the same prominence. The culprit for this is s.84 of the 1973 Act. In practice, the issue that will figure most prominently in most inquiries will be competition, but as Le Quesne points out, "the language of s.84 means that there is no limit to the matters which may have to be considered in relation to the public interest."[26] Changing the public interest criterion to give greater prominence to competition would be a major step towards ensuring greater consistency in the MMC's deliberations.

[25] Hay, D. and Vickers, J. 1988: The Reform of UK Competition Policy. *National Institute Economic Review*, August.
[26] Le Quesne, Sir G., 1988.

[108]

Critics of the MMC's deliberations in the BA/ BCal case feel that BA's claims that the merger would lead to greater efficiency, and that it would strengthen the company's standing as an international competitor, were given too much weight. Reversing the burden of proof would make it more difficult for firms to impress the MMC in this way. It would also force firms to back up such claims with more solid evidence. Another criticism, that the MMC did not give consideration to alternative solutions to the financial problems facing BCal, such as take-over by another airline, misses the point that as the law stands, the MMC (and OFT) is not asked to consider whether some alternative solution might be preferable to the merger under investigation. The MMC's duty is simply to consider whether or not the merger under investigation can be expected to operate against the public interest. Wider considerations of optimal market structure are beyond its remit. Similarly, the MMC is not able to take account of the possibility that a particular merger, though in itself acceptable, may trigger off others, and lead to an unacceptably high level of concentration. This is an unsatisfactory feature of existing merger policy, which deserves careful reappraisal.

Whenever an MMC report comes in for heavy criticism, a call is usually made for a radical overhaul of the whole system. In particular, attention is drawn to the fact that, apart from the Chairman, the Commissioners' posts are part-time. It is argued by some that the speed and quality of decision-making would be improved if investigations were conducted by full-time "professionals." In addition, a merging of the functions of the MMC and OFT into a single body has been suggested. A great deal of the workload of the MMC, however, is carried out by full-time staff, and their efforts may, for certain specialized tasks, be reinforced by the use of consultants. At least as important as the fact that commissioners are part-timers is the number and composition of the investigating panel. Typically, there are five or six members on any one investigation, and one of them will be an economist. It is quite possible for the views of one member to dominate, and for the conclusions arrived at in a particular case to depend on who happens to be on the investigating panel. It is considerations such as these, rather than the part-time nature of appointments, which give most weight to the call for a merging of the MMC's and OFT's functions.

The merits, or otherwise, of merging these functions is a complex issue which in part hinges on how widely the public interest criterion is drawn. As things stand, the OFT makes fairly extensive preliminary inquiries, focused on the extent to which a merger seems likely to increase market power. If there appear to be real dangers, the Director General will recommend referral to the MMC for a full investigation. The MMC will then consider not only the competition issue, but also

[110]

the efficiency defense, and any other matters which it considers relevant to the public interest. In these circumstances, there is much to be said for the existing division of duties. If, however, merger cases were to be decided on competition grounds alone, the case for merging the duties would be a strong one. The investigations carried out by the OFT do not form part of the MMC inquiry; the latter starts from scratch. The more narrowly policy is focused on competition issues, the more difficult it is to justify the existence of separate bodies weighing up the pros and cons of a merger using essentially the same sort of evidence.

DECISION-MAKING POWERS

It will be recalled that only the Secretary of State has the power to refer merger cases. In addition, following a referral, the MMC can only make recommendations. The Secretary of State decides at his discretion whether to accept those recommendations. This politicization of merger policy, and the concentration of power in the hands of one politician, has been criticized because it appears to diminish the authority of the Commission, and encourages lobbying, a practice much in evidence in recent cases, such as BTR/Pilkington, GEC/Plessey and Nestlé/Rowntree. Of the two – the power to refer, and the power to implement solutions – it is the former where the strongest case can be made for depoliticizing the decision-making process. Certainly, in practice, there have been several occasions when the Secretary of State has not taken the Director General's advice on a referral, but only once has the majority verdict of the MMC been rejected. If a merger bid is referred and the MMC's recommendations are not accepted, there is at least a great deal of information available on which to judge the issues. However, if the Secretary of State refuses to make a referral, there may be little information available by which to judge the wisdom of his decision. The case for placing the power to make a referral firmly in the hands of an independent body such as the OFT seems to be a compelling one. The issue of the power to implement solutions to merger problems is less clear-cut. Certainly it must be more difficult for the Secretary of State to ignore the recommendations of the MMC than it is for him to refuse to make a referral in the first place. Furthermore, there is the argument that it is right that the ultimate decision on whether the public interest should prevail over private rights should be taken by a minister answerable to Parliament.

In contrast, the EC draft regulation on mergers gives exclusive jurisdiction to the Commission. The Committee may find that a merger will create or strengthen a dominant position, but judge that this detriment is outweighed by one or more of the considerations outlined in Article 2(3), e.g., that it

[112]

improves the competitiveness of a sector in world markets. The Commission therefore would have the power to adjudicate not only on matters of competition, but on broad issues of industrial policy as well. Some observers believe that decisions on these wider issues at least should be made by a politically more accountable body.[27]

Conclusions

In spite of much criticism over the years, UK merger policy has changed little since its inception. Since 1984, referrals to the MMC are supposed to have focused more clearly on competition grounds, but referrals where competition is not the major issue continue to be made. In addition, the public interest criterion, by which the MMC judges the effects of mergers, has remained unchanged. The 1988 review made proposals for streamlining procedures, but not for any major alterations in the policy approach. The following changes, however, would arguably make UK policy more effective. Each suggestion is accompanied by a comment on the EC draft regulation.

[27] See Sir Gordon Borrie's paper, *National and EC Merger Control – Conflict or Peaceful Coexistence?*, presented to the International Bar Association, Berlin, 19 June, 1989. Sir Gordon is Director General of the Office of Fair Trading.

1 There should be a mandatory, rather than a voluntary, pre-notification procedure for all mergers above a given size. This would have the merit of ensuring that the OFT is fully informed of all important merger activity before the event. The provision of mandatory pre-notification in the EC draft regulation is to be welcomed.

2 The OFT should have the power to make referrals where the main issue is that of competition. The Secretary of State's powers of referral should be restricted to those cases where the main issues are other than competitive ones. The powers which the Commission has in this regard are appropriate.

3 The increased emphasis in the UK on referring mergers on competition grounds only is an improvement. Even so, referral procedures are still ill-defined. "Competition grounds" is a nebulous concept, and there is no publicly-known set of guidelines for referring mergers. The EC approach of challenging mergers that create or strengthen a dominant position is more precise. However, the criteria suggested for determining dominance could be given greater precision.

4 Efficiency benefits should be a permissible defense, but the burden of proof should be reversed, with the parties to a merger having to demonstrate that the merger would be in the public interest. If anything, this point applies with even greater force to merger policy at the Community level. After all, only those mergers with a

Community dimension, and which pose the most serious threat to competition, will be challenged, and if the policy of maintaining effective competition is to be taken seriously, it is surely right in these few cases that the burden of proof should rest with the parties to a merger. At the EC level the argument for placing the burden of proof on firms is further reinforced by the fact that the possible grounds for exemption in Article 2(3) have been very widely drawn.

5 In the UK, policy decisions are made by the Secretary of State, who is accountable to Parliament. Since the prevention or modification of a merger proposal involves the suppression of private rights, there is a strong argument to support the "politicization" of merger policy at this decision-making stage. The proposal in the EC draft regulation, however, gives these powers to the Commission, which is a much less accountable body. It has been argued that the Commission's powers pose a particular danger to competition policy because of the wide scope of the efficiency defense: in particular, for those cases where the Commission felt that a merger with anti-competitive effects should be allowed to proceed because of offsetting efficiency benefits, it should have the power only to make recommendations to the Council of Ministers. It is debatable, however, whether the Council is likely to adopt a more pro-competitive stance than the Commission. It is also no less likely to be interested in mergers

[115]

which the Commission has found to be anti-competitive and wishes to prevent. At least as important as who ultimately decides these cases is the way in which investigations are conducted – in particular the extent to which all interested parties are given a fair hearing, the scope of the efficiency defense, and who bears the burden of proof.

4

Knowledge Resulting from Merger Policy in West Germany

E. KANTZENBACH[1]

[1] The author would like to thank Dipl.-Volkswirt Reinald Krüger for his helpful comments and supplements to this contribution.

4

Introduction

By virtue of its long cultural evolution, and high level of scientific and technical achievement, Europe has good prospects of holding its own in the world market against its principal competitors in North America and East Asia. It will only make the best of the opportunities available, however, if structural conditions provide the business community with incentives to constantly increase performance.

Such structural conditions include the constant pressure of competition, derived from external sources by means of free access to the single European market, and from internal sources by means of consistent competition policy. The merger between Daimler and MBB[2] recently completed

---

[2] For details, see *Monopolkommission* 1989a: Sondergutachten 18 (Eighteenth Special Report). *Zusammenschlussvor-*

in West Germany makes particularly clear how strong the forces promoting concentration and restricting competition in the economy are nowadays. We can thus scarcely afford to refrain from mobilizing any forces that will tend to promote competition in the economy.

For this reason, we should certainly welcome the fact that the EC Commission has – after several failed attempts – again submitted a proposal for Community merger control.[3] Without this additional instrument, European competition policy would inevitably remain incomplete, and thus largely ineffectual. Even today, a growing number of corporate mergers may be observed in Europe.[4] Companies are pursuing this method in order to adjust to the single European market and to anticipated changes in competitive conditions. This threatens to hinder the desired intensification of competition accompanying increased integration.

---

haben der Daimler-Benz AG mit der Messerschmitt-Bölkow-Blohm GmbH.

[3] For the different proposals, see Ruppelt, H. J. 1989: Der Verordnungsentwurf für eine europäische Fusionskontrolle im EG-Ministerrat, 39 *Wirtschaft und Wettbewerb* 187, and *Monopolkommission* 1989b: Sondergutachten 17 *(Seventeenth Special Report). Konzeption einer europäischen Fusionskontrolle,* chapter IV.

[4] For example, see Jungnickel, R. 1989: Unternehmensstrategien im Binnenmarkt. In Mayer, O. G., Scharrer, H.E., and Schmahl, H. J. (eds) *Der Europäische Binnenmarkt* 96.

Moreover, a continuation of the present, highly divergent merger policies of the various member countries would distort competition in the single market.[5]

There appears to be unanimity among the member countries at present concerning the necessity of a single Community merger policy. There is less consensus, however, about the form European merger control should take in detail. The most controversial point is whether control should be exclusively concerned with competition, or also take into consideration industrial policy goals. The former view is currently maintained by Great Britain and West Germany, the latter especially by France and Italy.

This question seems to be significantly more important than the next most controversial issue, namely, the criteria within which cases come under Community control, rather than remaining within national jurisdiction. The position taken by the individual member countries on this second issue obviously depends on the extent to which they have succeeded in establishing their respective views concerning the criteria to be employed. The

[5] For an overview with regard to different approaches of national merger policies in member countries of the European Community, see OECD 1984: *Merger Policies and Recent Trends in Mergers;* Wullaerts, L. et al. 1988: *Merger Control in the EEC;* and *Monopolkommission*, 1989b, at Tz. 11.

greater their success in this regard, the more they are inclined to give jurisdiction to Community authorities, and vice versa.

In the following, I would like to discuss three problems affecting German merger control which are, in my view, also important for the discussion of European control:[6]

1   I would like to say something about practical aspects of the intervention threshold.
2   I would like to go into the problem, already mentioned, of additionally considering public interest criteria in connection with mergers.
3   I would like to comment briefly on the subject of delegating interventional powers to particular authorities.

1 The Competitive Intervention Threshold

Since its enactment in 1967, the German law against restraint of competition has contained, as its most essential competition policy instruments, a

---

[6]   In July 1989, the Monopoly Commission submitted a special report entitled "Concept for European Merger Control." The views expressed in this report largely coincide with my own. *Monopolkommission*, 1989b.

general prohibition against cartels (section 1), with possible exceptions (sections 2–8), and supervision of market-dominating companies to prevent abuses (section 22). In its basic structure, it corresponds to this extent to the competitive policy provisions (Arts. 85, 86) contained in the Treaty of Rome.

Merger control was introduced by amendment in 1974. The intervention threshold was adopted verbatim from the abuse control regulations. The Federal Cartels Office must prohibit any merger which results in or promotes a *market-dominating position*, unless major improvements in competitive conditions simultaneously occur (section 24, paragraph 1). However, the introduction of an additional definitive criterion, referred to as "paramount market position," and of definite concentration ratios as rebuttable presumptive criteria, has actually resulted in a substantial lowering of the intervention threshold. In assessing this intervention threshold, it is important to distinguish sharply between its application to horizontal mergers, on the one hand, and to vertical and conglomerate mergers, on the other.

The application to *horizontal* mergers has been substantially facilitated by presumptive criteria. These provide that market dominance is to be presumed when the market share of one firm reaches one-third. In the case of oligopolies, market dominance is presumed if the three largest suppliers have a market share of one-half, or if the five largest suppliers have a market share of two-thirds and no

[123]

substantial competition exists among the members of the oligopoly in their internal relations.

Although the presumptive criteria do not relieve the Cartels Office of its duty to thoroughly examine and evaluate all the circumstances of a merger, they have greatly influenced the decision-making practices of the Office and of the courts. Thus, in the first few years, the Office dealt almost exclusively with horizontal mergers, and its prohibitions were strongly oriented to the presumptive criteria.[7]

In my opinion, European merger control should also contain quantitative presumptive criteria as aids in establishing evidence and formulating decisions. I therefore regard their deletion from the draft regulation of November 1988 over that of July 1988 as a step in the wrong direction.

In regard to the level of the intervention threshold, it is difficult to come to a well-founded view. The extensive empirical material concerning the correlations between market structure and market performance allows only limited conclusions:[8]

[7] See *Monopolkommission* 1976: Hauptgutachten 1974/5 (First Main Report): *Mehr Wettbewerb ist möglich*, Tz. 909.
[8] For an extensive and current survey, see Schmalensee, R. 1989: Inter-Industry Studies of Structure and Performance. In Schmalensee, R. and Willig, R. D. (eds) *Handbook of Industrial Organization*, vol. 2, 951, North Holland. Earlier, see Scherer, F. M. 1980: *Industrial Market Structure and economic performance*. Chapter 9 (2nd edn) Boston:

1 It deals almost exclusively with the United States and, because of different institutional conditions, is not transferable without qualification to Europe.

2 It concerns almost exclusively price–cost ratios, i.e., the allocative efficiency of the markets. However, it appears that the constant improvement of products and production methods, and of corporate cost discipline, are much more important for the overall economy. However, hardly any meaningful empirical studies concerning the parameters of these market performance criteria are available.

3 The studies focus on linear correlations, from which a definite threshold value for market dominance cannot be derived.

Experience with German merger control does not justify the conclusion, however, that an intervention threshold of one-third market share is grossly mistaken. The threshold is significantly higher than that of the 1968 merger guidelines of the US Department of Justice, which are nowadays generally deemed to be too low. Given the new merger guidelines of 1982 and 1984, the threshold hardly allows of comparison, due to the different measures of concentration.

Houghton Mifflin. See also Kantzenbach, E. and Kruse, J. 1989: *Kollektive Marktbeherrschung*. Chapter 5 (1989).

If one takes into account the fact that geographically relevant markets within the scope of European merger control will presumably extend present national markets, then a market share of 20 to 25 percent – as provided for in the Commission's proposal of July 1988 – does not appear implausible. It is important, however, that geographical market definition in individual cases is based on thorough economic analysis, and that the territories of the member countries will not be mechanically assumed.

The most noteworthy result of more recent industrial economic studies is, in my opinion, the observation that above average profits result less from concentrated market structures, than from high individual market shares.[9] Obviously, the oligopoly problem was overestimated. The possibility of implicit collusion appears to be bound to very narrow preconditions.

This conclusion also accords with experience gained from German merger control. The Federal Cartels Office has often had difficulty proving collusive behavior, even in narrow oligopolies.[10] In the 1980 amendment, the burden of proof in this

[9] See Kantzenbach, E. and Kruse, J., 1989, chapter 5.
[10] See *Monopolkommission* 1978: Hauptgutachten (Second Main Report) 1976/7: *Fortschreitende Konzentration bei Grossunternehmen*, Tz. 419; and later see *Monopolkommission* 1982: Hauptgutachten (Fourth Main Report) 1980/1: *Fortschritte bei der Konzentrationserfassung*, Tz. 610.

[126]

regard was therefore reversed (section 23a, paragraph 2). Companies must now prove that, despite their planned merger, competition within the oligopoly will continue to exist. In view of the empirical data currently available, however, I have considerable doubts as to whether special statutory presumptive criteria are still justified in order to establish the existence of an oligopoly.

Within the scope of German merger control, the assessment of *vertical* and *conglomerate* mergers has proved much more difficult. The law expressly provides for their control. In determining market dominance, section 22, paragraph 1, subparagraph 2 requires that, in addition to market shares, the financial strength of the companies involved, their access to sales and procurement markets, interlocking relationships with other companies, and barriers to the market entry of other companies, be taken into consideration.

The Monopoly Commission has urged from the beginning that these provisions be extensively interpreted.[11] In its view, the market power of companies is based on superior financial and technological resources, as well as a large market share. This so-called "resources theory" is not uncontroversial, either in competition theory or in legal practice.[12]

[11] *Monopolkommission*, 1976, Tz. 909.
[12] For a critical discussion in Germany, see, for example, Möschel, W. 1984: Finanzkraft und konglomerater Zusam-

At the Commission's suggestion, a number of additional presumptive criteria concerning the creation of market dominance by means of vertical and conglomerate mergers were added to the law in 1980 (section 23a, paragraph 1). These criteria have hardly influenced the Federal Cartels Office policy, however.

Roused by Daimler's take-over of AEG, which was unopposed by the Federal Cartels Office, the Monopoly Commission then proposed in 1986 that mergers exceeding a certain absolute size be prohibited *per se*, and that approval be granted only in exceptional cases for public interest reasons.[13]

Personally, I am completely in favor of this proposal. Based on experience with German merger control, I see no other possible way to check the wave of conglomerate mergers that is now appearing in Europe. I realize that US competition

---

menschluss. *Die Aktiengesellschaft* 29, 257; Harms, W. 1985. In Benisch, W., et al. (eds) *Gesetz gegen Wettbewerbsbeschränkungen und europäisches Kartellrecht: Gemeinschaftskommentar/Begr. von Müller-Henneberg, H. und Schwartz. G.* Rz 452; and Dirrheimer, M. J.: Ressourcenstärke und Abschreckungswirkung in der Fusionskontrolle. *Neuorientierung des Wettbewerbsschutzes* 137 (FIW-Schriftenreihe H. 120).

[13] *Monopolkommission*, 1986: Hauptgutachten (Sixth Main Report) 1984/5: *Gesamtwirtschaftliche Chancen und Risiken wachsender Unternehmensgrössen*, Tz. 461.

authorities take a fundamentally different view of vertical and conglomerate mergers, and do not oppose them.[14] Many of our European colleagues also see in them the effectiveness of a workable market for corporate control rather than a form of competition restraint. The Monopoly Commission, however, does not share this view. I do not think the controversy over this issue has reached a conclusion yet. The Monopoly Commission's proposal, therefore, has no chance of being realized at present, either in West Germany or in the European Community.

2 The Consideration of Public Interest Criteria

The question of whether, and to what extent, other criteria, in addition to competitive criteria, should be taken into consideration by European merger control represents the core of the dispute among the member countries. These criteria could be derived from industrial policy, from general economic

[14] "As a practical matter, however, mergers not involving a combination of actual, direct competitors have been of virtually no interest to the Department of Justice since approximately 1982." Briggs, J. DeQ. 1988: An Overview of current Law and Policy relating to Mergers and Acquisitors. *Antitrust Law Journal*, 546, 693.

policy, or from the public interest, however that may be defined.

In national merger control, as currently practiced, we also find fundamental differences among EC member countries. In Great Britain and in France, mergers are assessed according to whether they are in the public interest or not.[15] This involves examining their supposed effects in various respects, e.g., their influence on employment, the trade balance, or the supply of consumer goods. The influence of competition is only one of these many criteria, and all of them are examined at the same time by the same authorities, and weighed one against the other.

In West Germany a different concept has developed, strongly oriented to American anti-trust policy. According to this view, general economic interests are best served by means of effective competition. Maintaining competition is therefore the predominant goal of competition policy, and hence of merger control. Only in exceptional cases can a merger which leads to market dominance be approved for public interest reasons (section 24, paragraph 3). This requires a decision by the Federal Minister for Economic Affairs.[16] Merger

[15] Within the national merger control of Great Britain, the "public interest" approach is different to that of the French control. See *Monopolkommission*, 1989b, 17.

[16] For a discussion of the public interest decision by the Federal Minister for Economic Affairs, see Knöpfle, R. 1974:

control is otherwise in the hands of the Federal Cartels Office, which is largely independent of political influences, and whose decisions are subject to judicial review.

Among competition lawyers and competition economists in West Germany, there is widespread mistrust of any government policy regarding industry structure. Many authors even maintain the view that the possibility of deciding on the basis of public interest in merger cases is more harmful than beneficial.

Based on my experience of the cases examined by the Monopoly Commission, I cannot share this view. There certainly are cases in which corporate mergers are appropriate for general economic reasons, although they restrain competition. In my opinion, the Federal Minister for Economic Affairs has also made only sparing use of his authority thus far.

I therefore do not agree with the German administration's view (or that of the British government), according to which public interest should play no role in European merger control. I can only explain this view as arising from concern over

---

Gesamtwirtschaftliche Vorteile eines Zusammenschlusses und überragendes Interesse der Allgemeinheit als Zulassungskriterien. *Wirtschaft und Wettbewerb* 24, 5; and Kantzenbach, E. 1986: Der Einfluss des Staates auf den Wettbewerb aus der Sicht der Monopolkommission. In Röper, B. (ed.) *Der Einfluss des Staates auf den Wettbewerb*, 39.

an excessively liberal approval policy, such as is practiced in France.[17] Furthermore, the German administration probably also expects that, even without explicit definition in the regulations, sufficient industrial policy aspects would be given consideration in the individual decisions. Apart from this, the position of the German administration has hardly become more convincing since its approval of the merger between Daimler and MBB.

In my opinion, there are important reasons which lead economic regulatory authorities to overestimate the industry policy advantages of a merger, and to underestimate the competitive disadvantages:

1 The advantages are often expected as a once-only boost, occurring relatively soon after the merger, while the disadvantages take effect in a form less noticeable at first, but longer-lasting. This is typically the case when economies of scale are achieved by means of a merger which also restrains competition. It is then only a question of time until the economic advantages of rationalization are more than offset by the long-term losses of efficiency caused by restraint of competition.[18]

---

[17] See Kleemann, D. 1987: Das neue französische Wettbewerbsrecht. *Wirtschaft und Wettbewerb* 37, 634; and Tonke, C. 1988: Das neue französische Wettbewerbsrecht im ersten Jarhr seiner Anwendung. *Wirtschaft und Wettbewerb* 38, 952.

[18] See *Monopolkommission*, 1989b, Tz. 102.

2 The advantages of a merger often accrue in a concentrated manner at the involved companies, while the disadvantages are widely spread, and thus escape notice. Good examples of this are mergers aimed at saving jobs, which are also frequently and emphatically encouraged in West Germany. In such cases, one company facing bankruptcy is to be taken over by another competitively strong company. What is often overlooked here are the reasons why the one company, and hence its jobs, are in danger. If it has failed to rationalize early enough, the new owners will inherit its problems, and probably have to eliminate jobs. If there is excess capacity in the industry, then preserving the capacity of the jeopardized company will drive another company into the position of being a marginal supplier. Its jobs will then be jeopardized, instead of those of the rescued company. The cautious assessment of such cases by the Monopoly Commission thus does not result from any failure on its part to rate employment goals highly. It results instead from the experience that corporate mergers are only seldom suitable to serve the goal of securing employment.[19]

3 The economic theory of politics teaches us that the economic policy of democratic states tends to give greater consideration to the interests of

[19] The Monopoly Commission has examined the question of securing employment by corporate mergers in the cases of Karlstadt/Neckermann, Babcock/Artos and Kaiser/Preussag/VAW. *Monopolkommission*, 1978, 10, Tz. 452.

producers than to those of consumers.[20] We can observe this phenomenon almost daily in all EC member countries. It is attributable to the fact that citizens are better organized in regard to their interests as employees or as entrepreneurs, and are more likely to prevail in these capacities. The welfare effects of workable competition, however, typically accrue in the more widely dispersed form of improved consumer goods supply. They are therefore likely to be neglected in the interplay of political forces, if they are not emphatically represented by an independent competition authority created for this purpose.

For the reasons mentioned, I think one should follow the Monopoly Commission, which in its latest report on European merger control takes a position in the middle. The Commission maintains the view that control should be essentially competition-oriented, and proposes market dominance as the threshold of intervention. Provided certain prerequisites are fulfilled, however, possible rationalization advantages should also be taken into consideration in merger assessment.[21] Such prerequisites would include that competition not be completely eliminated by the merger, and that the rationalization advantages of the companies in-

---

[20] For an overview, see Frey, B. S. 1981: *Theorie demokratischer Wirtschaftspolitik*; and Kirsch, G. 1983: *Neue Politischer ökonomie* (1983).

[21] *Monopolkommission*, 1989b, Tz. 102.

volved be passed on to their customers. Beyond this, however, general industrial policy goals and public interest benefits should not be taken into consideration.

This view largely accords with previous positions taken by the Monopoly Commission. Corporate mergers can facilitate rationalization measures, i.e., more efficient organization of procurement, production, and distribution, and promotion of research and development. In such cases, the general economic advantages of a given merger are recognizable and assessable by the deciding authority. This is not the case, however, when mergers in restraint of competition are to be justified by reference to general economic goals, or to the general objectives of the Treaty of Rome. Such findings are practically no longer verifiable, and thus open up unlimited possibilities for political opportunism.

3 The Institutional Organization of Merger Control

In West Germany, there are, in extreme cases, up to four institutions involved in the decision-making process.

A merger is first examined by the Federal Cartels Office, as to whether it will lead to, or reinforce, a market-dominating position. This purely competitive examination is then subject in its entirety to judicial review. In many cases, the courts have revised the Office's decisions. The Federal Cartels Office is, in a formal sense, a subordinate authority of the Federal Ministry of Economic Affairs, but in all individual decisions it enjoys virtual judicial independence.

If a merger is prohibited for competitive reasons, the companies involved can apply for approval based on reasons of economic policy or public interest. Next, the politically responsible Minister is the competent authority for this decision. He must weigh the restraints of competition determined by the Federal Cartels Office against possible public interest advantages. This is a political, discretionary, decision, and is consequently not subject to judicial review. In order to make this decision as objective and transparent as possible, the Minister must obtain an expert opinion from the independent Monopoly Commission before making his decision. This opinion is published immediately, prior to the Minister's decision.[22]

This is, admittedly, a very circumstantial and costly procedure. In my opinion, however, it is justified, and has proven its worth. It takes into account, to the greatest possible extent, the points mentioned above, namely that conflicts between

---

[22] The most recent expert opinion by the Monopoly Commission was made for the Daimler/MBB case. See *Monopolkommission*, 1989a.

competition optimization and rationalization regularly arise in connection with corporate mergers, and that government regulators are exposed to considerable one-sided political pressure to decide in favor of producer interests, and against competition.

The division of decision-making authority at least ensures that controversial mergers are examined thoroughly in accordance with competitive criteria, and that the results are made known to the public. The Minister is not restricted in his freedom of decision, but is still subject to considerable pressure to justify his action.

Based on my experience, a two-stage process of merger control seems desirable for Europe. If the creation of an independent European Cartels Office, as proposed by the Monopoly Commission,[23] is not feasible, at least the competitive and the industrial policy assessment of mergers should be made independently of each other by different directorates general, and be published. This would provide the Commission with the basis for a balanced final decision.

[23] *Monopolkommission,* 1989b, Tz. 137.

Index